Construction project teams:

making them work profitably

'The tree is also aware of its environment to an astonishing degree.
It maintains constant awareness and the ability to adjust itself in two
completely different worlds, so to speak — one in which it meets little
resistance in growing upward and one composed of much heavier
elements into which it must grow downwards' (Roberts, 1979)

Construction project teams:

making them work profitably

Tim Cornick
& James Mather

Thomas Telford

Published by Thomas Telford Publishing, Thomas Telford Ltd, 1 Heron Quay, London E14 4JD

URL: http://www.t-telford.co.uk

Distributors for Thomas Telford books are
USA: ASCE Press, 1801 Alexander Bell Drive, Reston, VA 20191-4400
Japan: Maruzen Co. Ltd, Book Department, 3–10 Nihonbashi 2-chome, Chuo-ku, Tokyo 103
Australia: DA Books and Journals, 648 Whitehorse Road, Mitcham 3132, Victoria

First published 1999

A catalogue record for this book is available from the British Library

ISBN: 0 7277 2745 1

© T. Cornick and J. Mather & Thomas Telford Limited 1999

Typeset by KeyWords DTP, Brighton
Printed and bound in Great Britain by MPG Books Ltd, Bodmin

Preface

Like the tree shown in the frontispiece, construction project 'teams' are naturals — and have been so for thousands of years. Their members come together continually on 'one-off' projects which are large or small, simple or complex, and, with minimal instruction, perform their own role in conjunction with others instinctively. However, they currently have to grow from a recent tradition that contractually often sets them at odds with each other inadvertently — and certainly offers no positive encouragement that everyone's effort should be financially rewarding for having taken part. This book offers views that can be taken in construction project management which — while still having to cope with the recent traditional environment — may help produce profitable teamworking.

The challenge in writing this book is to focus all of what is currently understood about how human beings work best in teams in the context of a construction project. To do this it will be equally important to define both the nature of human teams and the nature of construction projects, and how one impinges upon the other. Neither can the impact of emerging *information* technologies be ignored, as these will influence in the near future how team members can best communicate with each other during the course of a construction project. As traditional and new ways of procuring construction projects will also influence how members behave towards each other, these also need to be taken into account in teamworking. Finally, the fact that each project comprises not only *individual human beings trained in different disciplines* but also a group of *very diverse businesses* must also be considered in achieving effective teamworking.

The underlying approach to this book has been to take 'theory' of human organizations, especially teamworking, and map it to the design and construction process at five levels of process analysis. Construction project 'teams' comprise different people who are formally appointed to carry out different types of 'specialist' work in a certain order from inception to completion. This 'team' therefore has to operate at the following levels:

- human (people type to people type)
- operational (discipline work process to discipline work process)
- information (knowledge data to knowledge data)
- organizational (business firm to business firm).

Although current conventional wisdom would stress the importance of the first, *human* level for teamworking, the other three levels cannot be ignored — especially in the way they impact on the first. Each chapter in Part 1, after the Introduction, considers these levels through a focus on a particular theme, each viewing the construction project team as:

- a unique generic process and composition
- diverse people and cultures
- diverse disciplines and stakeholders
- diverse business firms
- a temporary organization
- an information exchange.

The case studies in Part 2 provide a vehicle by which 'theory' can be related to the issues of 'practice'. The five case studies cover a spectrum of types and sizes of construction projects including building and civil engineering works. The case studies are linked by their reviews to the key point summaries of each of the 'theory' chapters.

This book sets out to address teamworking in terms of a '*construction project* team'. The influence of the *project* — which is unique and has a defined beginning and end — combined with the activity of *construction* — which has its own peculiarities compared with an other 'production' activity or 'type' of project — on the 'teams' of human beings that take part as representatives of business firms is significant. Unless *all* of these levels are considered and managed both *individually* and *interactively*, it is unlikely that an construction project team will find itself engaged in *profitable* teamworking.

NOTE ON TERMINOLOGY

Throughout this book we refer to the participants in a construction project team by their *function*, as such a book is concerned with *processes* which comprise the *work* that people do and how they do it. This means that in using the terms *designer, construction manager* and *specialist trade contractor* we are *not* advocating construction management as the only method of procurement that supports effective 'teamworking'. It does, however, mean that whatever form of procurement is used – either in its purest form or in some sort of combination – the recognition of *function*, rather than a *legal position* of 'architect', 'engineer', 'contractor' or 'subcontractor', is the foundation for effective teamworking in a construction project.

ABOUT THE AUTHORS

Tim Cornick is an architect by profession with 10 years' experience in the design and contract administration in both public and private practice in the UK and New Zealand prior to being appointed a research fellow and then lecturer in construction management at the University of Reading in 1979. During his career as an academic he specialized in research into quality management, construction project management and computer-integrated construction. He has taught these and related subjects at masters levels and on short courses for industry, and has presented papers at international conferences in these subject areas. He has won and managed seven major government/industry jointly funded research contracts and teaching company schemes to a value of £0·75 million. He has also had two books published by international publishers in the subject areas of quality and computer-integrated construction.

Currently, he is a visiting research fellow at the University of Reading, and director of The Loddon School and LIAISE, which provide residential care and education for children and young people with autism, and is co-director of the TEAMIT Training Programme – a joint academic/industry endeavour to ensure university-based continuing professional development (CPD) training meets the needs of busy people in practice. He is a member of the International Alliance for Interoperability, which is an international industry-based organization that promotes future interoperable computer systems between all construction disciplines. He is also the UK representative of an EU project looking at the harmonization of construction project management training and recognition between member states.

James Mather is a senior partner of Johnston & Mather, a small firm of architects and project managers founded in 1980. Johnston

& Mather undertakes high-quality residential, conservation and educational architectural work in the UK, and educational, infrastructure and medical/institutional work in Romania. For the past 3 years, the firm has also been involved in training architects, engineers and other professionals, in partnership with the University of Reading.

He is a Past-Chairman of the Register of Engineers in Disaster Relief (RedR), an organization which selects, trains and supplies engineers and other technical experts to the major agencies operational in disaster relief. RedR runs about 17 training courses annually on technical and management subjects. He is also Chairman of BLIZZARD and a trustee of the Ungureni Orphanage Trust, organizations active in eastern Europe in the support of educational and community development, and also development of institutional standards for the care of the handicapped. He is an occasional lecturer at the University of Bucharest, at the invitation of the Romanian Ministry of Education. He has recently been awarded an MBA at the University of Reading.

Both authors are co-directors/tutors of a CPD course in construction project management for all construction disciplines held at the Department of Construction Management and Engineering, University of Reading.

Contents

1. Introduction   1

Part 1   **19**
2. Joining the project team — the business case   21
3. A construction project team — its nature and
    problems   33
4. A team of diverse people and cultures — dealing with
    the differences   60
5. A team of diverse disciplines and stakeholders   72
6. A team of diverse businesses — meeting collective
    business objectives   85
7. A team as a temporary organization — getting the right
    arrangement   103
8. A team as an information exchange — communicating
    the right messages   115

Part 2   **127**
9. Case study: the railway at Berzozil   129
10. Case study: Alminster Old Town Hall   148
11. Case study: the Ark, Hammersmith, London W6   157
12. Case study: Argent House   167
13. Case study: Kelso Day Centre — a self-build scheme
    for the homeless in east London   176

Part 3   **185**
14. Conclusion   187

Appendices   **193**
1. Personal styles   195
2. Training programme   201

References   **215**

Index   **219**

1

Introduction

WHY THE CURRENT CONCERN FOR 'TEAMWORKING' IN CONSTRUCTION?

From the 1960s to the 1990s a succession of UK government-sponsored reports has exhorted the construction industry to 'work better together' in order to improve its productivity and performance. The separate responsibilities for design and construction inherent in traditional procurement methods (Joint Contracts Tribunal, 1960 onwards) have been seen to be one problem that needed to be addressed and solved. This is because of the perceived 'adversarial' type of contracts required by these methods. Another major factor that was seen to be needed to be addressed and solved was how to cope with and effectively exchange the vast amount of information created during the course of a project. This was essentially through emerging information technology tools through computer applications.

The UK construction industry has also been subject to the veritable onslaught of new management concepts that has happened to all other industries over the last 20 years or so, from quality assurance via BS 5750 in the early 1980s on through to total quality management, business process re-engineering and a current host of new 'management' concepts that appear almost month by month. 'Teams' and their 'leadership' have now become the current concern of management across all industries, the construction industry included. How teams form and perform in order to meet the aims of *any* business and the needs of the 'customers' they serve is now uppermost in the minds of academics and practitioners alike.

The *construction* industry also has some distinct features in the way it goes about its business, which means it cannot be exactly compared with *manufacturing* industries in its practice. These differences impact upon 'teamworking' and how and why it is applied. To begin with, modern building or civil engineering construction has become complex enough as a 'product' to warrant a wide range of design and construction organizations becoming involved throughout the project life cycle. Seldom could it be said that any one organization is solely in charge of the construction project process at any one time. The commissioning client, or its appointed project manager, relies entirely on others to be in charge of the design and construction process with both activities more often than not being the distinct responsibility and liability of separate business organizations.

These many separate organizations working in close harmony over quite often a long period of time are fundamental to the overall business of construction. The construction industry, as a whole, is very fragmented and does not dictate how its own market might develop in terms of producing its 'products' for 'customers'. Its 'products' are only needed when its 'customers' in the form of individual clients ask for them on a 'one-off' basis. These individual clients then usually need them to be produced as fast and cheaply as possible, having regard to a specific quality standard to meet a particular client's own business needs. Being able to form 'teams' of not only *people* but also *organizations* as rapidly as possible in order to perform to the highest standard in the fastest time is therefore vital to the very nature of any construction project.

Two of the latest reports regarding construction, *Constructing the Team* (Latham, 1994) and *Trusting the Team* (Bennett and Jayes, 1995), both stress the 'team' theme by their title, if not entirely by their content, the former becoming most noted for its challenge to the industry to be able to reduce the cost of construction by 30% by working better together, and the latter by promoting the virtues of and defining the requirements for 'partnering' between client, construction and design organizations as a means of overcoming traditional 'adversarial' contracting on either a long-term corporate basis or a project by project basis.

So, then, the notion of *working together better* and all the benefits that it should bring to the client, design and construction organizations alike is at the heart of the current desire to understand and apply 'teamworking' to the construction project process.

2

INTRODUCTION

WHAT ARE 'TEAMS' AND WHEN DID THEY FIRST APPEAR?

Like many 'hot topics' today, there is nothing new about human beings working together in teams to achieve a common goal. When early man started to hunt something that was bigger than any one person could handle he started to do it with others. The hunting party was a group with a very important common goal — to obtain food to survive. However, it was not just the sheer weight of numbers against the prey that was important but also that, almost instinctively, the group brought together a collection of different 'skills' — such as spotting, tracking, chasing and making the kill — the combination of which made the hunting party that more efficient and effective and reduced the risk of injury or death to the hunters during the course of the hunt.

Very soon man, through his aggressive nature, started 'hunting' himself to satisfy not so much the need for survival but more the quest for power and the recognition that the power over others would bring. The *hunting* party became the *war* party that still practised the same combination of skills but for a more sinister reason. Also, these early 'teams' produced their own natural 'leaders' by virtue of the one who was the physically strongest, the bravest and, probably, the most quick-witted. Although armies grew and warfare became an increasingly complex art and technological science right up to the modern day, the well-led, highly skilled and committed infantry platoon may still be the basic 'team' that brings ultimate 'victory' in a war between combating sides.

Construction itself probably generated the earliest example of 'teamworking', for more peaceful purposes, as man emerged from the caves and started building his shelters from natural materials on top of the ground. As societies grew larger, got more organized, established 'civilization' and developed 'religions' so the constructions man created became not mere 'shelter' or 'service' but symbolic and monumental — and by definition much larger and more complex in their design and construction. So long-term planning and organization of how natural materials would be found, removed, brought together and erected to form structures according to a *designed plan* — from megaliths to pyramids — gave us the earliest examples of major construction projects in which large groups of people had to work together over long periods of time to achieve a common goal. In many cases the participants had no choice, and many died, but the power structures of these civilizations enabled a committed elite to exercise the power to make them happen.

Although most effort was in the sheer physical muscle of vast numbers of people moving heavy material components, specific skills started to emerge, in both *design* and *construction* activities – with the architect (that is to say, the person that both *designed* the finished building and *planned* its construction) being the overall 'leader' of the 'team'. The 'team' by now was becoming extremely large, with many 'subteams' all with their own 'subleaders' (many of whom used whips as motivators!) carrying out different tasks – for example excavating the stone from its natural place, and transporting it to the construction site.

Teams, tasks and individuals, some committed, some coerced, under leadership of one sort or another but mostly 'dictatorial', therefore all started to emerge very clearly and very early on in the evolution of civilized man in the context of the construction process. It might therefore be argued that the construction industry – if 'industry' could be defined as man organizing himself in groups to produce something by collective effort – is the oldest and most *traditional* of all industries. This might be the reason why it seems to be the slowest to change on the one hand, but on the other hand has always had to deal with the relationship between 'team', task, individual and leadership. All of which is the basis of the 'three circle needs' model suggested by modern organizational theorists (Adair, 1983).

So, then, teams under leadership, and all that entails in human and organizational terms, have been with us since the beginning of the time we see man emerging from being a primitive creature seeking basic shelter and food to survive. Construction 'industry' teams are as old as the structures they left behind as their 'product'.

HOW DO 'CONSTRUCTION TEAMS' ESSENTIALLY DIFFER FROM TEAMS IN OTHER FIELDS OF HUMAN ACTIVITY?

All teams comprise people working together to achieve a common goal. This can be at work or at play, and quite literally so in terms of the soccer team who all work together to score more 'goals' than the other side in order to win their match. What is reputed to be the world's most popular sport provides a simple yet very clear example of what teams are all about and how they work, in that in the soccer team:

- every individual has a vested interest in the team winning
- each individual provides and applies very distinctly valued but necessarily related skills
- the team is 'led' by someone who plays and can inspire the rest by being there on the field of play

- the team is managed by someone who does not, or usually does not, play but understands the game and sees the overall picture from the side and can provide all necessary resources
- they all train together in order to understand and plan how all their individual contributions can come together as a whole team effort.

Construction project teams vary from this 'ideal' in that:

- every individual has a vested interest in their own firm 'winning' — which may or may not be the same as the project team 'winning' unless shared 'goals' are obvious and accepted
- each individual provides and applies very distinct personal skills — but not necessarily very obviously valued or even very related
- it is not obvious who is actually 'leading' the project team as this might vary over the life of the project and the 'inspiration' of the 'leader' is seldom felt by every team member because it is not obvious who he or she is or where how and where he or she is 'playing' in the team
- the *project manager* does appear to be someone who does not, or usually does not, play a part in either the design or the construction process but, however, understands them both, and sees the overall *project process* from the 'top' but cannot necessarily provide all the 'time and cost' resources that the rest of the team would like
- owing to pressure of time, cost and convention they seldom all train together for the specific project and only understand and plan how all their individual contributions can come together as a whole team effort in a very *ad hoc* manner as the project progresses.

Construction project teams also vary from other teams in other industries, or other companies that provide some sort of a service, in that, as a whole, they comprise individuals who are employed by different firms that are very different *businesses*. For example, an architectural practice and a small specialist joinery firm are very different businesses but their individual people need to be a part of the 'project team'. Construction project teams, more often than not, come together for just one project having never worked together before and with no guarantee of ever doing so again. Depending on the length of the project, the particular key team member from any one firm may also change during the course of the project. During the *design* phase the team may stay reasonably stable in terms of people and firms. However, during the *construction* phase the people and firms can change quite frequently as the various trade or package contractors join, complete their work in sequence and then leave.

Partnering approaches (Latham, 1994; Bennett and Jayes, 1995) recommend long-term relationships between *client, design* and *construction* organizations as a means of overcoming many of the perceived deficiency problems caused by some of the above factors. However, in the majority of cases, a long-term strategic 'partnering' approach may not be possible for very practical reasons. For example, only a few major clients who continually build could guarantee an ongoing construction project programme to its design and construction 'partner' firms. 'Partnering' on a project by project basis would be more applicable for widespread industry application and the mechanisms of this approach are reviewed in subsequent chapters.

So, then, construction project teams are, by their very nature, most fluid in terms of people and most diverse in terms of firms and often have unclear 'leadership' and agreed specific goals, seldom train together and come and go on a project by project basis.

WHEN DO 'PROJECT' TEAMS COME TOGETHER IN CONSTRUCTION?

A construction project develops or evolves through some very distinct phases. Whether described by a plan of work (Royal Institute of British Architects, 1968 onwards) or a construction management procurement process (CSSC, 1991) the basic generic phases it passes through are:

- *briefing* — during which the project requirements are identified
- *designing* — during which design solutions are proposed and agreed
- *specifying* — during which the production requirements are defined for the physical realization of the design
- *tendering* — during which prices for the production are determined and agreed
- *constructing* — during which the production is carried out
- *maintaining* — during which the completed project is managed for its useful life.

Ensuring that all the 'requirements' of everyone involved are clearly identified and that it is agreed that they have been met throughout every one of these phases as a 'chain of conformance' is the aim of any quality management process for a project (Cornick, 1991). The above six phases also describes the outline life cycle of a project.

The formation of the construction project team throughout these project phases can be considered as follows, as described by basic 'functional' (but not necessarily 'contractual') roles:

- *briefing*: client/project manager (as *briefer*) and designer (as *design* advisor) + construction manager (as *construction* advisor)
- *designing*: client/project manager (as *design* approver) + designer (as *designer*) + construction manager (as *construction* advisor) + specialist contractor (as *specialist designer*)
- *specifying*: client/project manager (as *design/construction* approver) + designer (as *detail designer* approver) + construction manager (as *construction method* advisor) + specialist contractor (as *specialist design construction method* advisor)
- *tendering*: client/project manager (as *construction price* approver) + designer (as *design* monitor) + construction manager (as *construction management pricer*) + specialist contractor (as *specialist construction pricer*)
- *constructing*: client/project manager (as *construction* monitor) + designer (as *design* monitor) + construction manager (as *construction manager*) + specialist contractor (as *specialist constructor*)
- *maintaining*: client/project manager (as *facility manager*).

It is useful to point out at this stage that not only is the client/project manager likely to be 'pluralistic' (Green, 1996), that is to say having more than a single individual and more than a single interest involved, but the same will also apply to the designer, construction manager and specialist contractor. It is also useful to point out that these 'functions' are *always* carried out on *any* project regardless of whether the procurement route is traditional, design and build, or construction management or 'any' hybrid of all three. The procurement method only changes the *context* and *relationship in time* in which these functions are carried out. How this affects teamworking will be addressed in later chapters.

So, then, construction project teams come together over the life of the project with the role of the same team member changing as each phase comes into being. The client/project manager is there at the beginning and the end of the project throughout all its six phases.

WHERE DOES 'TEAMWORK' TAKE PLACE IN A CONSTRUCTION PROJECT?

In all other manufacturing industries and other service enterprises 'teams' by and large are formed and work in the same place, for example the factory, office, school or hospital, and even though some 'outside people' are brought in from time to time for various reasons, the *place* remains the same. Even the soccer team has its 'home ground' at which it feels at a greater advantage than when 'playing away'!

The opposite is true of the construction project team, whose 'place' of working can change as the project progresses through its phases from a range of offices of different client interests, consultants and regulatory statutory undertakings to the construction project 'site', which itself becomes the place of production and final operation in use. Even during the constructing phase, the client/project managers, designers, construction managers and specialist contractors (who have to do some 'off-site' production) may all be still carrying on part of their work in their own place.

So, then, by its very nature, a construction project team is a 'virtual' team where people have to work together but from very many different locations over the life of the project. The significance of this fact is picked up on in later chapters as it has a major impact on interteam communication in terms of information exchange in each project phase.

WHO ARE THE 'TEAM MEMBERS' AND WHO 'LEADS' THEM?

As described previously, the construction project team comprises four distinct participants in terms of professional or trade disciplines, firms and, by definition, types of people.

The first is the *client/project manager*. The client commissions the project and can be either a public or a private organization, with an 'in-house' or externally appointed project manager who represents the interest of the commissioning client. In terms of 'leadership' it is the client/project manager that has the highest overview of all the requirements of the project and is in the best position to give overall direction to its evolution.

The second is the *designer*. The designer is responsible for the overall design and construction solution for the project's 'end product' in terms of the construction's form, structure, fabric and other engineering systems. In terms of 'leadership' it is the designer who has the highest overview of the 'end product' design for appearance and performance and is in the best position to give overall direction to the construction's design.

The third is the *construction manager*. The construction manager is responsible for assembling the human and physical resources needed to realize the 'end product' through coordinating the efforts of the designer and the specialist trade contractors. In terms of 'leadership' it is the construction manager who has the highest overview of the physical construction process and is in the best position to give overall direction to the design's construction.

The fourth is the *specialist trade contractor*. The specialist trade contractor is responsible for the final assembly of a particular element, system or 'package' of construction and in the majority of cases is responsible for the particular detail design. In terms of 'leadership' it is the specialist trade contractor who has the highest overview of the particular construction part and is in the best position to give overall direction to its detail design, off-site manufacture and on-site assembly.

The team role terms used above best describe their function and would be the actual contractual roles if the construction management method of procurement was employed. If the traditional method was used then the construction manager would be put in the role of *main/general contractor* and the specialist trade contractor in the role of *subcontractor*. With the design/build method the construction manager would have the role of *design/build contractor*, the specialist trade contractor the role of subcontractor and the designer, if not 'in-house', the role of a subcontractor designer.

In all the methods, the client/project manager would be carrying out the same function and role and the designer would most likely always be a consultant architect or engineer or a team of both. It also goes without saying that in all but the very smallest of projects, all the above four team functions would each comprise a 'team' themselves.

So, then, each team member has a very clear and distinct function and practical relationship which may be affected, one way or another, by the method of procurement role they have to fulfil. With regard to 'leadership' of the construction project team it would appear that for very practical functional reasons it can 'shift' according to which function is dominating at any particular time. However, the overall project would most practically be 'led' by the client/project manager, being the function that has the highest overview of the project as a whole.

WHAT ARE THE FACTORS THAT INFLUENCE HOW WELL – OR HOW BADLY – A CONSTRUCTION PROJECT 'TEAM' CAN WORK TOGETHER?

Like any group of people brought together to carry our any task of whatever sort and for however long, a number of factors will influence how well – or how badly – they work together and operate effectively as a 'team'. It has been suggested (Chang, 1994) that to have a *dynamic* team in any organization the team needs to:

- clearly state its mission and goals
- operate creatively
- focus on results
- clarify roles and responsibilities
- be well organized
- build on individual strengths
- support leadership and each other
- develop a team climate
- resolve disagreements
- communicate openly
- make objective decisions
- evaluate its own effectiveness.

It would appear that many of the above elements are always naturally in place in any construction project. For example a *clearly stated mission and goal* would be to 'build a building, bridge or road' and each basic key team member, as described above, *operates creatively* for his or her own particular contribution to the overall design and construction process. Each of the project's evolutionary phases has definite enough outputs in terms of information or completed construction to make sure that there is a *focus on results* and, as also described above, each team member's *role and responsibility* is distinct and *clear enough*. It is true that, by definition, the *individual strength* of each team member is used and *built on* throughout the project and, through its traditional conventions, *disagreements are quickly resolved* to allow progress (although the ramifications can be felt long after in pursuit of financial claims). *Communication is reasonably 'open'* between all parties who have to communicate to carry on with their part of the project and *decisions are usually 'objective'* when all the relevant factors have been considered.

Those elements that may *not* necessarily be 'naturally' in place in any one construction project are, for example, that there are *unclear roles and responsibilities* beyond the basic functions of each team member; the project is not necessarily *well organized* as a 'team'; *lack of identity of and therefore lack of support for 'leadership'* as it shifts from one team member to another; an *undeveloped 'team' climate*; *'disagreements'* which although *'resolved'* in the short term have long-term costly consequences because they are not really resolved satisfactorily; and, finally, there is often no real opportunity or incentive for the 'team' to *evaluate its own effectiveness* as a whole and there are even 'liability' inhibitions to do so anyway.

The influences that may result in the latter elements *not* being in place are varied but will come from either human, operational, information, organizational or legal (contractual) factors. For example, the traditional method of procurement and the contractual systems which support it can well inhibit 'team' *effectiveness evaluation* because of individual party's 'liability' consequences. Equally, an ill-thought-through information system with any method of procurement can seriously inhibit *open communication* and therefore indirectly affect *mutual support* in terms of 'knowledge sharing' when it is needed. All of these 'inhibitors' are considered in the following chapters of this book, along with how they can be removed to allow a construction project team to become dynamic so that all the 'team' can work together more effectively, efficiently, enjoyably and, most importantly, economically.

So, then, the elements that are considered to be needed to make a *dynamic* team that will work together well are in part always there in any construction project. Those that are *not* are those that are inhibited from being so by the way the project is structured and managed on a number of different levels.

HOW CAN CONSTRUCTION PROJECT 'TEAMWORKING' BE IMPROVED?

The construction industry is constantly under re-examination as to how its work can be improved. As previously stated, recent reports all start to point towards the belief that this 'overall improvement' will come in part through utilizing changing 'technologies' and in part through improved 'teamworking'. In the author's view (Cornick, 1996) the twin 't's of technology (whether new construction or information technology) and teamworking (brought about by new management approaches) are interdependent in the context of achieving overall improvement in the industry's performance, in whatever terms that improvement may be measured.

11

Improving the 'teamwork' part, just like improving the 'technology' part, will come initially through knowledge about what these approaches are and how they relate to the industry's current structure and practices. Change in any field of human activity is never that revolutionary, in that change itself inevitably means changing the 'status quo' from which the majority of people in work derive their economic and emotional security. Change is therefore initially resisted until those people whom it will affect can see it as an opportunity and benefit rather than a threat and disadvantage.

The construction industry — and those who work in either the design or the construction firms which it comprises — is no exception to resistance to change and, perhaps because of its traditional historic roots as an 'industry', is more resistant than most. However, its people, whether designers or constructors, are by the very definition of their work very practical and therefore often sceptical of 'new' ideas — technological or managerial — unless the advantage is very obvious — preferably in the short term and they can see how it will help them on their next project!

Given the basic need for a construction 'team' to have to work as an interdependent group anyway, it might be argued if the right 'environment' is created to allow improved teamworking, it will naturally happen! What will be important, however, is to show how the techniques that address these missing elements can be applied to the individual 'team member' — designer or constructor — in their relationship with another 'team member' in the context of the overall construction project.

So, then, improved teamworking will come when certain missing elements are understood, and permitted to be applied, by each team member in the context of their day-to-day work — that is to say in working on a construction project.

WHY WILL PROJECT 'TEAMWORKING' IMPROVE THE 'BUSINESS' OF THE DESIGN OR CONSTRUCTION ORGANIZATION?

Much government-sponsored research has been promoted in the UK and EU to determine both managerial and technological ways in which the construction project process can be improved to the benefit of the client. In practice, in the UK, the construction management method of procurement was applied by leading property clients as they found that the method could save them 25% on the overall cost of their projects. Both in practice and research the focus has been on the benefit to the *client* of new approaches — essentially through lower costs, faster times and higher quality standards — with benefits to the other project team members not necessarily being the priority.

This focus is not surprising seeing that it is usually the client who determines which way the construction industry's 'supply side' — that is to say the designer (architects and engineers), construction manager (contractors) and specialist trade contractors (subcontractors) — delivers its construction 'product'. This is because the client, and especially the large powerful client, determines the project and its financial arrangement and is therefore in a strong position to challenge the industry's own 'status quo'. Another problem is that the 'supply side' is somewhat disintegrated in terms of overall organization so that the designers are 'professional consultants' and the construction managers/specialist trade contractors are commercial contractors — each with its own 'business' agenda. In the eyes of many clients, the architects and engineers are still being used as 'professional watchdogs' over the contractors and subcontractors, and this is a relationship which is reflected in the spirit of the traditional contractual systems.

Efforts to integrate all participants in business terms is fraught with traditional stances and attitudes and it is only when a design/build deal is offered to potential clients that any sort of integrated business commercial approach comprising both the design and the construction responsibility comes into effect. Even then the 'partnership' between the professional consultant designer (architect/engineer) and commercial construction manager (contractor) may only last for the duration of a single project, with the client still being outside the 'partnership' in any business sense.

A partnering approach to a project may unite *all* the participants — client included — in some sort of a 'partnership' but not in the true sense of the word in business terms. Even then it will still only be for the duration of a project or series of projects.

Teamworking on a single-project basis therefore presents a major challenge in that *different* individuals with *diverse* skills and experience, all coming from *various* firms each with their own 'business' aims, have to work together *immediately*. Depending on the method of procurement, teamworking can be further challenged by the fact that different 'specialist' designers, the construction manager and specialist contractors may join the team one by one in sequence over a comparatively long period of time depending on the scale of the project. And even then, only through winning their place in the team in a harsh, competitive pricing environment by being the lowest tenderer — which increasingly can also apply to the designers as well as constructors.

So, then, the application of 'teamworking' techniques should ensure that everyone is working as closely together as possible as soon as a new member joins the 'team'. In this way all new individuals — and the firm's businesses that they represent — will be able to feel and practically experience not only being 'part of the team' but also that they are meeting their own 'business' needs through common objectives.

WHO HAS TO CHANGE THEIR PRACTICE AND HOW, FOR IMPROVEMENT TO OCCUR?

It goes without saying that as the construction industry's approach to projects has for so long been based on practices that often militate against effective 'teamworking' *every* participating member will have to change. How these practices need to change will depend on both each participant's current practices and the way these interact through the various methods of procurement. The necessary changes in practice could be defined as follows.

Client/project managers will need to see themselves, and be seen by others, as part of the project 'team' with a shared interest in the success of all other 'team members'. They will also be the ones who contributes the final key project decisions where design and construction management purposes may conflict.

Designers will need to see themselves as the 'team members' who generate creative solutions regarding the construction 'end product' for all other 'team members' to consider and agree. They will also be the ones who contribute the essential information for design decision-making.

Construction managers will need to see themselves, and be seen by others, as the 'team members' who generate creative solutions regarding the construction 'production process' for all other members to consider and agree. They will also be the ones who contribute the essential information for construction management decision-making.

Specialist trade contractors will need to see themselves as the 'team members' who generate creative solutions regarding particular 'end product and production processes' for construction elements for all other members to consider and agree. They will also be the ones who contribute the elemental construction and, in many cases, its detail design information.

14

The changes required therefore do not entail a change in any way of the basic functions of the individual team members but of the way in which they see themselves and are seen by others. It also means that instead of 'passing instructions' down the line from client/project manager to designer to construction manager to specialist trade contractor they 'agree requirements' with each other through the creative exchange of ideas. Above all, the change should ensure that *everyone* is valued by the others for the contribution they make to the project as a whole. What the import of this sort of change will be at the five levels of 'teamworking' operation outlined in the Introduction will be described in the following chapters.

So, then, change must be made by everyone in their view of each other and the acceptance of each others 'creative' ideas. It goes without saying that the project procurement environment in contractual, operational and organizational terms should support these changes in approach.

WHAT IS THE 'PAY-OFF' AND WHEN WILL IT BECOME EVIDENT?

The 'pay-off' must be financial in the first instance and will only come when 'teamworking' results in each business firm represented receiving the profit it expected when it priced for its work. This in turn will only happen if 'wasted time' or, even worse, 'rework' — which can be 'redesign' or 'reconstruction' depending on the team member's function — is minimized and altogether eliminated. The link between improved 'teamworking' and reduced wasted time and rework is that the former should, more than anything else, ensure *good communication always* and *the sharing and exchange of information at the right time* during the evolution of the project. This is because wasted time and rework have been shown through much applied research into construction management (Cornick *et al.*, 1988–1996) to be caused by miscommunication and untimely information exchange between project participants — essentially between designers and construction managers/specialist trade contractors.

A secondary business benefit to each firm involved must be that it allows it to deliver its particular contribution to the construction project — whether that contribution comprises design or construction — in the best possible light in terms of its reputation. Enhancing its reputation will attract repeat business direct from the client or through the recommendation of *any* other project team member. Delivering its particular contribution in the best possible light will only happen if what it has to deliver is absolutely clear and agreed in good time and that any change, for whatever reason, is acceptable by all the other team members affected. Assured repeat business also brings its own financial reward in the long term.

So, then, improved 'teamworking' will above all bring about improved *communication* between all team members who represent different business firms. This will minimizes the miscommunication that has been shown to be the root cause of all costly and financially unrewarding mistakes in the construction industry's process.

WHERE WILL THE FIRST SIGNS OF IMPROVEMENT APPEAR?

Applied research and practice development in construction management has endeavoured to show that *working together better* brings about improvement for everyone in a construction project. This working together better can be seen in a number of approaches. Changed methods of procurement that encourage clients, designers and construction managers to integrate their processes in the construction management method of procurement has been one (CSSI, 1991). 'Partnering' (CIRIA, 1997) on a project by project or strategic basis has been another. These early experiments, however, still reveal a need for the industry to change its interdisciplinary and interpersonal culture and improve its communication between project team members if these methods are to show real benefit.

One of the most interesting developments in construction procurement to improve teamworking has been the private/public partnerships in a number of different EU countries. This is called the Private Finance Initiative (PFI) method in the UK (HM Treasury Task Force, 1997), and consists of using private financing to fund public building or civil engineering projects. Here the 'team', which comprises designers, constructors funders and operators, all combine their efforts through a special company to provide public authorities with a service, for example a maintained road for a number of years for an accepted price (University of Reading, 1997–1999). In this method there is a clear financial benefit for everyone to work together to produce a construction on time to cost and a known standard. This is because they all can have an equity stake in the special company and even the client acts like a consultant to the special company that will provide the service for an annual payment.

Although it is difficult to demonstrate the exact measurable financial benefit of working in these ways compared to following the more traditional routes, because of the 'one-off' nature of every project, all the evidence suggests that they are there to be realized by each participating firm. These changed approaches are not necessarily bringing the hoped-for benefits that they should, because all firms that participate in them still have people employed that have been brought up in their working life using the traditional approaches. The mistrust and miscommunication potential that is inherent in those approaches is not easy to overcome in practising people's minds! It is also true that the vast majority of small to medium sized projects that the construction industry undertakes are not appropriate to these public/private partnership methods.

So, then, the first signs of improvement in practice — with *financial* reward — through *working together better* are already evident. These approaches and what makes them work which could be applied to *all* procurement approaches; how they work and how their workings relate to 'teamworking'; and how the real and lasting change in construction practice will come about will be described in more detail in later chapters and case studies.

IN SUMMARY

It can be seen than since the earliest times man has worked in organized groups to achieve common ends. Construction provides one of the earliest examples of this phenomenon and construction projects, of any reasonable scale, can never be realized *unless* a team of people with diverse knowledge and skills is created and operates together. Teamworking between different individual people from different firms coming together on a project by project basis is the natural order of things in the construction industry, but with each individual member also being involved in *other* construction projects. The traditional method of procurement has given all the people who practise throughout the design and construction firms that comprise the industry a particular mindset that is difficult to change immediately.

Poor teamworking on a project has a number of human and organizational causes, the effect of which is that, although the project eventually is completed, some of the participating firms suffer loss of profit or loss of reputation — both of which are bad for business! Improving construction project teamworking must therefore improve the business of the participating firms.

In human management studies there is a theory X and a theory Y (Adair, 1983) in which alternative 'assumptions about man' are made. In theory X the view is *negative* and suggests that 'man' needs to be coerced into working and working together. In theory Y the view is positive and suggests that 'man' can be encouraged into working and working together. Leaders will by and large take either theory X or Y as the basis for their own approach in leading their team. On the basis of the inherent nature of the construction project process previously described and the assumption that the vast majority of people who work for design and construction organizations match theory Y, this book proposes a *theory Y(T)*, which can be stated as follows:

- In general, man by nature is gregarious and wishes to work well in groups to achieve an end goal that is beneficial to each individual member. In particular, design and construction people and firms also wish, *and need*, to work well together as an effective project team — not only to satisfy their clients' needs but also for the benefit of themselves personally as well as their own businesses.

So, then, the remainder of this book, through chapters on theory and case studies that demonstrate the theory in terms of practical issues, will therefore establish what the current 'blocks' are that prevent this theory Y(T) being applied in practice at the human, discipline, business, organizational and informational levels — but, more importantly, how those blocks are best removed.

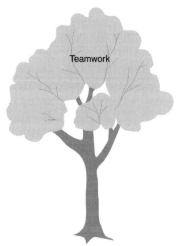

The construction project process

An improvement method. Addressing the key factors of the process to support profitable teamworking to support profitable teamwork

18

Part 1

2

Joining the project team — the business case

THE CLIENT'S 'BUSINESS' REASON FOR FORMING THE CONSTRUCTION PROJECT TEAM

In all but a very few cases the client has a very specific 'business case' for wanting a construction project. The nature of the 'business case' will depend on the nature of the client organization and the 'business' with which it is involved. The diversity of 'business' — and therefore the diversity of the 'business case' — will be essentially determined by the client organization's:

- provision of a type of *service* or a *product*
- *public* or *private* ownership
- unique business *method and culture*
- unique position in its *field and marketplace*.

The purpose of the project in business terms may be to either expand or improve either the service or the product provided by the client, which may or may not have a directly measurable financial benefit. It may be, in the case of the 'development' client, just a means of investing money in order to get a profitable return through sale or rent. Many major clients, who continually construct, begin their projects with a 'business case' in order to ensure that all the future design and construction management proposals can demonstrate they satisfy such business criteria (IAI, 1997–1999). So, in the first instance, the client organization's 'business needs and expectations' set the foundation

21

and framework for the construction project's 'business case' and supporting business methods.

A construction project will, by definition, absorb financial resources *of* as well as having a some sort of disruptive effect *on* the client's ongoing business organization — especially in the case of construction alterations and additions to an existing site or building already in use. It may be the case that the most critical criterion to be satisfied in a client's project is how the existing business might remain fully operational for the project duration, with the actual design and construction criteria being secondary. Even a public organization, whose sole purpose is to construct — for example, a highways authority — and which has its own 'budget' which it cannot exceed in any particular financial year and has to balance funding for new works with maintenance, has to consider the 'business case' for each project in its own right. This means that the prudent client organization will need to formulate at the very outset of a project a 'business plan' for the organization that demonstrates the needs, methods and implications of the construction project.

A 'business plan' for a *construction* project can be mapped from a recognized 'business plan' for any new business start-up or project that is concerned with an existing business expansion (Cohen, 1994). The 'business plan' framework that describes the client's company would be as follows:

(1) organization details
(2) summary — background and belief
(3) activities — what is 'produced' (either a service or a product, or both), where and for whom
(4) history — of the area and company members
(5) marketplace and marketing
(6) competition
(7) personnel
(8) direction of market
(9) strategy and plans — how the company's 'product'(either a service or a product, or both) is going to be 'produced' it terms of pricing and technology
(10) financial forecasts:

    (a) projected profit/loss account (1–5 years)
    (b) overheads projected (1 year)
    (c) projected cash flow (1 year)
    (d) projected balance sheet (1 year)
    (e) notes on projections:
        (i) repayment profile

(ii) creditors

(iii) prepayments

(iv) accruals

(v)   assets (plant, equipment, etc.).

Having mapped the client's *company* 'business plan' for the project on to the project itself, each element of the plan can be defined in terms of the project's unique characteristics. For example, there will be a part of the company's *organization* that will be particularly concerned with the project, the *background and belief* may have a particular significance for the project, the specific *activities* of the company will have a major impact on the project's design brief and so on.

However, it is the *financial forecast* for the project that will have the most immediate impact on the client company's business. From a business point of view, raising the finance for the project through loan, grant or – in the case of charities – donation; when it is acquired related to when it has to be paid out, and when it has to be paid back in the case of a loan; and how all these transactions fit into the ongoing company cash flow are crucial. Only if this all works *financially* can the project be considered viable and therefore the project team be formed at all.

The business plan itself should also inform the client on the right procurement strategy to adopt. For example, a public authority client might decide for budgetary reasons to follow the 'public/private partnership' route to avoid any capital expenditure. A private client might chose a construction management approach so that each participant can be individually chosen for quality reasons and for a known cash flow of expenditure. And so on. The procurement method will, by and large, then determine how the design and construction team member firms will be selected and their ongoing financial relationship with the client.

Unless the client's representative on the team, who will now normally be a project manager, feels confident that the company's resources are readily able to afford the project, he or she may find him- or herself subconsciously acting in a 'negative' way – if only to try and save the company's money as the project proceeds. If the client representative is, by either design or default, taking the team leadership role then the whole project team will be adversely affected by that attitude.

So, the business case for the client company must be demonstrably sound if the contribution by the project team member is to be 'positive'. The only reason why the client project team member may start to be 'negative' will be if he or she has the feeling – either real or imagined — that the project cannot really be afforded. Therefore, if that is the case, there will be the temptation to act in a way that exploits every possible weakness in the project process to the financial disadvantage of other project team members.

THE DESIGNER'S 'BUSINESS' REASON FOR JOINING THE CONSTRUCTION PROJECT TEAM

The remaining members of the project team have different 'business' reasons from that of the client for joining the project team. It is self-evident that the reason why building and civil engineering design and construction organizations actually exist at all is to take part in construction projects. That is, construction projects that are set up by clients wishing to have a building or civil engineering 'product' outcome. If, as they may well do, design and construction organizations establish their own projects — as a development venture, for example — then in effect they are the 'client' also, even though they may have in mind another 'end-user' client (see Chapter 10 for an example of this type of situation). However, the usual situation is that design, construction and other cost or management organizations are 'in business' to provide a service to a client — public or private — who wishes to have a building or civil engineering construction, the 'project' being the process by which the final construction is realized.

Although all these organizations have in common the fact that construction projects are their 'business', design organizations have different motivations from the others. There is also another difference because architects and engineers, apart from being 'designers' for the project, have also traditionally provided the client with 'professional advice' regarding the whole construction process. For example, they tend to have the duty to help select the organization to carry out the construction of their design and then administer the contract on the client's behalf. The description of these organizations as 'consultants' who are paid a 'fee', rather than 'contractors' who are paid a 'price', also denotes a traditional perception that differentiates them from the other organizations involved in the project team. It might even be considered a deep-rooted 'class' distinction.

Design organizations essentially comprise architects and engineers or multidisciplinary organizations combining both, who, by definition, wish to 'design' and be creative in their work and the means by which they earn their living. They are usually professional practice partnerships, as opposed to limited-liability companies (although some practices have moved in that direction more recently), and as such have been inhibited, until quite recently, in aggressively 'marketing' their services to potential clients. Although as 'businesses' they have to have the objective to make a profit to stay in business, their prime motive for taking part in any client's project is the opportunity it provides for them to design. This can be because either the type of project involves the sort of building or civil engineering works for which they have become 'specialists' through experience or it provides an opportunity to branch out into a new design field. Often their first involvement may be through winning a public design competition. It is probably true to say that their prime 'business' motive in taking part in any client's project is to enhance their reputation as designers and professional consultants — and usually in a particular specialist area of construction type and architectural or engineering style.

The business case for these organizations is therefore based on the desire to first and foremost be creative in construction design and, to that extent, use the client's project as a vehicle to achieve that end. In a business sense it could be argued that design organizations are in business to 'design' either buildings, specialist engineering elements of buildings or civil engineering works, and that their 'designs' are what they sell as a business. Although these 'designs' are 'one-off' and in response to a particular client's specific set of requirements, the purpose of these organizations, both commercially and culturally, is to be architectural or engineering designers. Their purpose is 'vocational' and in one sense any 'commercial' motivation is secondary. As they come to the project to meet a client's specific need they will tend to be reactive rather than proactive as a business organization.

The greatest 'business' risk for the design firms is that in their enthusiasm to be given the opportunity to design they may not seriously fully consider their own business case for taking part — especially in terms of the cost of their human resources. The fact that design itself is evolutionary may make it very difficult to accurately judge just how long it will take to get to the point where it fully satisfies all the client's requirements. Comparisons with similar projects may help in this judgement but the uniqueness of a particular client's project may only help in arriving at a crude idea of resource needs.

The realization once the project is under way that their quoted fee may not in the end cover their costs, let alone show a profit, may start to inhibit architects' or engineers' positive contributions as project team members.

THE CONSTRUCTOR'S 'BUSINESS' REASON FOR JOINING THE CONSTRUCTION PROJECT TEAM

Those organizations that provide the physical construction of the design in a project can be considered as:

- main and general contractors, who manage the overall construction process carried out by specialist trade contractors as *sub-contractors* as a commercial contract or construction managers, who do the same as a professional service to clients with the specialist trade contractors as direct contractors
- specialist trade contractors, who assemble the elemental parts of buildings and civil engineering structures, either as subcontractors to a main contractor or direct contractors to the client.

Both of these, as businesses, generally respond to an invitation to construct a design generated by the design organizations to meet the client's project brief. The invitation can be either through direct competitive tender in competition with similar organizations or through negotiation, either in competition or not, or without any competition through direct 'partnering' between themselves and the client's organization (see Chapter 3). As with the designer's organizations, these construction organizations are experienced in, and to an extent motivated by, the desire to construct buildings or their specialist elemental parts. It can further be argued that the specialist trade contractors are very focused in terms of the 'technology' they work with and its cost, whilst the main contractors or construction managers have the wider organization of construction and its overall cost as their work expertise.

Their business success depends on their financial ability to predict and control the cost of overall construction or specialist elemental parts, respectively, and in relationship to the price they have given in a winning tender or negotiation. Because of the 'one-off' nature of clients' projects, the accurate 'prediction' of the construction cost of a hitherto unknown design is the challenge for these organizations. More so for the main contractor/construction manager than the specialists for whom, because of the very nature of their specialist work, *elemental* costs may be easier to predict, regardless of the needs of the particular construction design. This is especially true because the specialist trade contractors may often be required to do the detail design of the element they are going to construct.

26

The business case for these organizations is therefore based on their need to be comparatively competitive, yet profitable, in their tender or negotiation pricing for a particular design for a particular client's project, and then on their ability to control their cost during the actual construction. In a business sense it could be argued that the construction organizations are in business to 'construct' — either buildings, specialist engineering elements of buildings or civil engineering works — and that 'constructed designs' are what they sell as a business. Although these 'constructed designs' are 'one-off' and in response to a particular client's specific set of requirements, the purpose of these organizations, both commercially and culturally, is to be architectural or engineering designers. Their purpose is primarily 'commercial'. As they come to the project to meet a client's specific need they will be *re*active rather than *pro*active as a business organization.

The greatest business risk for the construction organizations is that as the construction phase of the project evolves the price they have contracted to build for starts to appear not to cover their costs — let alone give them their hoped-for profit. The outcome of this is that they will start to seek claims for extras, which may or may nor be justifiable. Once a 'claims' culture develops, this not only takes up valuable time as the client's project manager and designers start to resist the claims and question their justification but starts to create a negative atmosphere and inhibits a positive relationship between all the team members.

THE COST AND PROJECT MANAGER'S 'BUSINESS' REASON FOR JOINING THE CONSTRUCTION PROJECT TEAM

Organizations that provide cost management for the client — 'quantity surveying' practices in the UK — and, more recently, organizations that provide independent *project* management also have their own 'business' reasons for joining the construction project team. These may differ in detail from those of the design and construction organizations.

Traditionally, cost management organizations have been recommended by architects to help manage the project's design and construction costs on behalf of the client as a separate project participant team member. Their appointment is a 'professional' one and, like the design organizations, they receive a fee for the service they provide. The actual work they essentially carry out in providing this professional service comprises setting cost targets, measuring general construction work in order to obtain agreed rates of construction, monitoring the evolving design against cost plan targets, monitoring costs and changes during construction and agreeing the final costs at the end of the project.

More recently, project management organizations have been appointed by clients, often at the inception of the project, to provide an overall 'professional' management service to the client to ensure that the client's cost, time and quality standard requirements are met. This service, which has evolved for *building projects* over the last 20 years in the UK, is perceived by many clients, especially *public* clients, as being the means by which all the other project participants — that is to say essentially the design and construction organizations — are managed *together* in the client's best interests.

Both of these types of organization have in common the fact that they directly provide *neither* the 'design' *nor* the 'construction' for the client's project. What they therefore have to 'sell' to a client is an assurance that the professional services they provide will mean that all the client's interests — especially its *financial* interests — are looked after in the total project process.

The business case for these organizations is therefore based on the desire, first and foremost, to be professionally supportive in achieving the client's overall project objectives. In a business sense it could be argued that these cost and project management organizations are in business to 'assure' clients who want either buildings or civil engineering project objectives met, and that their 'project objective achievement assurance' is what they sell as a business. Their purpose is 'vocational' and in one sense any 'commercial' motivation is secondary. As they come to a project to meet a client's specific need they will tend to be *reactive* rather than *proactive* as a business organization.

MARKETING FOR THE 'SUPPLIER ORGANIZATIONS' INVOLVED IN THE CONSTRUCTION PROJECT

The above organizations coming to the project can be considered as either the 'customer organization', which is the client's, or the 'supplier organizations', which are the remainder. It can be said that in terms of business:

- the 'customer organizations' see the project as the means by which their own business will be improved or expanded

- the 'supplier organizations' see the project as a business opportunity for their particular work skill, knowledge and experience

but that in the widest possible sense *both* have similar generic 'business' objectives to be met in common through the project. That is to say the result of the project should improve their financial position and enhance their reputation in their particular marketplace.

However, it is the 'supplier organizations' that have to seek out clients in order to continue their business, which is solely dependent on clients needing projects. The only change to this situation comes if the design and construction organizations decide to create building or civil engineering projects — possibly in partnership with other financial and operational organizations — themselves for either sale, lease or some other form of payment. However in this situation it could be argued that these organizations have become part of the 'client' organization itself.

'Supplier organizations' seeking project work will need to market their services in such a way as to ensure they find clients *who are considering* a construction project. The sooner any organization can become involved in a client's project the better if it is to perform well as a project team member. This will allow it both to help develop the evolution of the project and to give it a greater understanding of its own involvement in terms of its own resources, and hence its costs related to its price and fee and the expected 'profit' to its business. Although this early involvement is most necessary for the *project management* organization, it must also be advantageous for *design, cost* and *construction management* organizations. In certain circumstances, key *specialist trade contractor* organizations who make a major contribution towards the design will find it a business advantage to have an early involvement in the project.

Marketing for any business entails certain key principles, most of which will be applicable to the 'supplier organizations' to a construction project (Frith, 1997). Of particular note if the organization is to be part of a high-performing team for the benefit of both the client *and* the organization's own business are the following:

(1) The 'supplier' organizations should have business plans for the continuance of their own businesses and these should inform them as to the type of client's project they should be seeking to join.

(2) Their knowledge of their marketplace needs to be detailed, and although in general terms it is 'construction', in project terms their market may be very specific, for example a particular type of client.

(3) Marketing is a structured method to implement the firm's business plan so that its business goals are achieved (which could be breaking into a new type of client project market) and is the direction and focus of actions to achieve business goals.

(4) The importance of marketing is to ensure that any project management, cost management, design or construction firm has a profitable revenue stream (which just one inappropriate project could adversely affect, especially if the project is a large one and the firm a small one!), the firm's resources are effectively and efficiently used and not wasted, and it is prepared for the challenges of competitors and changing needs of its marketplace.

(5) On the basis of the firm's business plan (previously described in this chapter), a marketing plan should have been drawn up and followed, comprising at the very least:

(a) marketing *objectives* for focus, resources and targets

(b) marketing *analysis* comprising a study of the social, economic, political and technical factors affecting the market, trends and their combined effect on future business prospects

(c) a marketing *audit*, which would look at such things as market size, share, segments (for example, in the construction market, the 'newly privatized' client organizations), growth, opportunities and threats, ending with market prioritization for attractiveness.

(6) The outcome of the marketing process should be a clear picture for the firm of its marketing mix of 'product' (which in most cases would be a 'service'), 'package', 'placement', 'price' (which will determine the fee it should ask for from any prospective client) and 'promotion' (especially of a 'professional' service) in obtaining a place on future clients' projects.

Unless each of the 'supplier' firms to the project has gone through such an exercise for its own firm then it might find itself on the wrong project with the wrong client, and other 'supplier' organizations losing money and reputation! And this will not be conducive to positive teamworking for the client's project. Marketing for all business firms is a subject in its own right and readers are advised to study it further as it is crucial to their business of working on construction projects (Armstrong *et al.*, 1996).

IN CONCLUSION

The business case for each the organizations joining the construction project team is:

- for the *client* organization, a very specific professional and/or commercial reason to increase or improve the service or product it provides in its unique place it holds in its particular marketplace — and which needs to be financially supported by a business plan
- for the *designer* organizations, a very specific professional reason to provide a design, and possibly construction advice, service for a particular client — and which needs to maintain and enhance their reputation for construction design in a current field or establish it in a new one
- for the *constructor* organizations, if they are:
  - *main contracting or construction management* organizations, a very specific commercial and/or professional reason to provide a construction service in realizing a given design for a client
  - *specialist contracting* organizations, a specific commercial reason to provide the construction, and sometimes detail design, of a specialist construction element;

  in both cases the reason needs to maintain and enhance the organization's reputation for either construction management or specialist contracting in a current field or establish it in a new one
- for the *cost and project management* organizations, a very specific professional reason to provide a project cost or management control service for the construction of a design for a particular client — and which needs to maintain their reputation for either cost or project management in a current field or establish it in a new one.

It is important for all organizations that take part in a construction project that the client's business case for the project is sound and appreciated — as this will inform everyone about priorities. It is equally important for each participating firm that its own business case is equally sound and it can reasonably deliver what it has promised. Both are necessary for harmonious teamworking. How the organizations that comprise a construction project team can function and succeed as a temporary 'business' together is described in detail in Chapter 6.

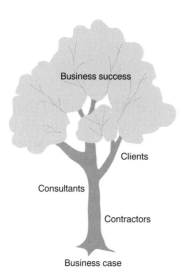

A business approach. Meeting the business needs of clients, consultants and contractors to support business success

3

A construction project team — its nature and problems

HOW ARE PROJECT TEAMS SPECIFIC IN CONSTRUCTION?

The construction project team has a purpose, composition and method of working which are unique to the industry it is formed to serve. This uniqueness stems from the fact that:

- its *purpose* is determined by a *client* who is not part of the *design and construction* supply side of the industry
- its *composition* in terms of firms (and subsequently their people) is not necessarily selected because of their ability to form an effective 'team' in human terms but because they propose the most technically and financially attractive *design* and a competitive price for *construction*
- its *method of working* is by and large based on the 'conventions' of how each separate type of client, design and construction firm carries out its normal practice through 'traditional' contractual arrangements formally and by a 'negotiated consensus' informally.

In other words, in other product or service industries the team that is formed for a 'project' — whatever that 'project' may be — does not start with above constraining factors. For example, and by way of comparison if an automotive firm wishes to form a project team to create a new product line, the 'team' will have:

- a *purpose* determined by the automotive firm itself on the basis of its extensive experience of the design, production and selling of automobiles
- a *composition* comprising team members who are mostly 'in-house', with the same company employer and presumably embracing the same company philosophy
- a *method of working* which has no 'contractual conditions' between each party and where working practices are not necessarily hidebound by a 'tradition' of how separate organizations usually work together, but can be appropriate to the particular project being undertaken on the basis of the company's own internal practices.

The implications of these constraining factors mean that *for a project team*, at the very least, a shared philosophy will have to be created which will entail breaking down barriers created by 'traditional' methods. And tradition dies hard! The 'organization' has to be created anew at the beginning of each project using people who are most likely unfamiliar with each other's specific working practices. Also, the fact that their entry into the project may well have been as a result of their firm having bid the lowest price for the work they have to undertake means that they will have to watch their time input. They may well feel compelled also to look for the chance to claim extra payment over their original price for their work at every possible opportunity — just to ensure that they do not make a loss, and preferably make the profit they expected to make when tendering.

However, in a *construction* project team, the uniqueness of purpose, composition and method of working can also be a benefit. Because of the 'one-off' nature of construction projects having regard to a particular combination of

- a *client* with a particular motive to construct and budget in mind
- a *type* of building or civil engineering work
- a *location* of geological, topological, geographical and man-made characteristics
- a *place* of sociological, political and economic 'climate'
- a *time* of year and duration,

the general focus of the project team's purpose can be very clear by reason of its uniqueness. That is to say that client 'A' has a motive, a budget 'B', a location and place 'C' and a time 'D', and this is the reason for the project and unique aim for the team's efforts. The project team's purpose, on the one hand, may be very obvious in the sense of providing a finished construction, but may be less obvious in terms of some of the client's 'hidden' motives and budget and time 'flexibility'. After all, most clients are aiming to get the *most* out of the supply side of the industry for the *least cost* and in accordance with *their own timescale* — which when combined with the other project factors might actually be totally unrealistic! The real purpose may therefore be hidden — either by default or design — from the majority of the project team, depending on the approach that the client chooses to adopt. And clients can be extremely wide-ranging in their enlightenment about the construction project process and how the best all-round performance can be obtained from its teams.

The uniqueness of the construction project, as defined by the above combination of factors, also impacts as both a benefit and a disadvantage on the *composition* of the team. It goes without saying that all construction project teams, regardless of project type or size, *comprise specialists* who all have a very obvious general role to fulfil. That is to say:

- the *client* provides the brief, the budget and the site
- the *architect as designer* provides the overall architectural solution to the final construction
- the *engineer as designer* provides the specialist engineering solutions for the building's elemental parts
- the *contractor as construction manager* provides the overall organization of the physical resources need to realize the design solutions
- the *specialist trade contractor* provides the physical elemental parts for the design solutions and, in many cases, much of their detail design.

The general composition of the project team can be very clear by reason of the traditional functional roles required for any project. However, by contrast, the very uniqueness of the project may mean that selecting each specialism by virtue of its specialist function *only* may *not* meet the particular combination of project factors. For example, the uniqueness of the project may demand a particular *architectural style* as the most appropriate design solution — but only certain *architects* might be inclined to create that style. So, too, might an individual *construction element* require particular expertise to satisfy the requirements of the overall architectural design solution, which may not be available from the *lowest element tenderer.* And so on!

The method of working by and between all members of the construction project team does, however, have a long tradition of how

the team's work will be carried out. This can be found in many professional 'codes of practice' (Royal Institute of British Architects, 1968
onwards) of how *one* team member carries out his or her work and in
'contractual systems' (JCT, 1960 onwards) which provide the basis of
how the construction 'contractor' carries out his or her work in relation
to the design 'architect' and 'engineer' and in relation to the client over
the project's various stages. As various sectors of the industry take on
more systematic methods of working through the adoption of quality
management systems (BS 5750/ISO 9000; British Standards Insitution,
1997), more generic methods of working emerge providing guiding
'frameworks' within which any construction project team could and
should work together during a project.

However, none of these generic methods will necessarily automatically produce the most appropriate methods of working to suit the
unique combination of project factors described above. For example, it
could well be that just the particular sociological and political climate of
the project could be so significant as to make 'traditional' methods of
working entirely inappropriate. The best solution for getting the
project done might be to base all the design and construction management solutions on the fact that only certain specialist trade skills are
available at a particular time. Or that, considering the remote locations
of various team members as the project evolves, setting up an
Internet-based method of communication right from the inception of
the project should be paramount and a key criterion for team firm
selection.

So, then, the uniqueness of the construction project team has some
clear benefits for 'teamworking' generally but may be constrained for
the purposes of really efficient 'teamworking' by the often hidebound
practices of the various traditions of individual team members and
contractual arrangements. In essence, a construction project team has a
purpose, composition and method of working that are generally very
clear but the danger is that the 'hidden' project-specific factors that will
greatly affect the efficiency of its process may be overlooked.

WHAT ARE THE 'ORGANIZATIONAL' PROBLEMS CREATED BY THE PROJECT'S 'TEMPORARY' NATURE?

Many researchers have studied the construction industry's process
from the point of view that each project is a *temporary* organization. All

of these studies point out the fact that the temporary design and construction organization does *not* have the following features that an efficient *permanent* organization (for example a school) may automatically have in place, such as:

- a *shared philosophy* about how the members go about their work
- an established *known 'customer' base* towards which all their efforts can be focused
- an *established organizational structure* of people and their responsibilities and relationships
- an *established set of work procedures* relating work in sequence to people and processes
- a *cost and pricing structure* for its service or product against which 'profitability can be measured
- a *marketing and business strategy* to ensure its long-term viability.

Unless *all* of these can be created very rapidly at the inception of the project, either some or all of these features will be lacking throughout the duration of the project. Perhaps the most important feature of any successful organization is a strong shared philosophy about what it exists for and why it will make a marked difference to the product or service 'market' it has been set up or evolved to serve. The organization's philosophy more often than not comes from a passionate belief held by either a single founder or a small group that something can be done better than it ever has before. Examples of this can be found in every field of human endeavour and it is the zeal which is at the heart of all social, political and religious systems as they reform and develop the way people live together in society over the history of human civilization. Sometimes for good but sometimes for evil. Many current national and international businesses — some in the construction field (for example MACE and Simons Construction) — are fundamentally successful because they are based on the foundation of a passionate belief in a particular way of doing things which is accepted by those who come and work, and stay, for the organization because of its shared philosophy.

The *permanent* organization has, above all, time to allow this shared philosophy to permeate as the organization grows owing to its own self-generated success in the particular market it serves, as it inevitably takes more of that market's share. With the construction project, the *temporary* nature of which is also an ever-changing as new firms join as work progresses, this time factor is extremely short or almost non-existent depending on the size of the project. If there is a philosophy to be held it must be held by the client/client project manager who is the only permanent member of the team and will be there from inception to completion of the project. The one advantage that the construction project as a temporary organization has over the permanent organization is the fact that it is created from new and that every project is a 'fresh start' for all team member firms working together. However, each firm must be prepared to 'buy in' to the project philosophy and its ability to do so should be as much a criterion for its selection as its price!

Each project has in effect its own unique customer, which is the commissioning client that pays for the work. The disadvantage of this is that the knowledge of that customer, and the environment that they operate in as a business in their own right, has to be rapidly acquired by the project team as a whole and as soon as possible. Even with clients who continually build, they may be constantly changing as a customer whose needs must be met because their own business environment is constantly changing. So, for example, education and health care clients have changed as customers over recent years as the way they operate has changed. For example, the hospital 'client' is no longer a regional hospital board but is now an individual hospital trust and as such is a different sort of customer for the supply side of the construction industry.

The very fact that the construction industry's customers are so wide-ranging in type and size makes the establishment of a known 'customer' base an impossible task. Each client, as a 'customer' who has needs to be met, has to be considered on a project by project basis as the real needs may vary even between apparently similar types of client. A further complexity in applying the concept of a known 'customer' base derived from the product or service permanent organization to the temporary construction project organization is that the client — in one sense the 'customer' — needs to be very much part of the team providing the construction 'product'. The client is both 'customer' and part 'supplier' in the construction project team.

The organizational structure of the construction project has been studied and portrayed by many researchers and is usually described in terms of roles (which are also contractual), responsibilities and relationships. Variations on the actual structure again can vary from project to project and lines of reporting can sometimes be confusing and changing, unlike those of a permanent organization. The simplest organizational diagram, and the one that best describes the construction management procurement method, shows the specialist trade contractors reporting equally to the designer and construction manager, who in turn report to the client or client project manager. In effect this is the best *functional* description of any project team, regardless of procurement method, in that the *purpose* of every participant is to provide a service or product to a commissioning client who pays. The only difference is that in other methods either the designer or the specialist trade contractor provides his or her service or product through a construction manager acting as an overall 'contractor'.

This arrangement best shows the reality of any project, in that dual reporting is always needed because there are always both *design* and *construction management* issues to be considered by all parties to the process. For example, as a specialist trade contractor develops detail design solutions to a particular elemental part of the construction, the solutions must satisfy both the overall design concept produced by the designer and the construction plan and programme produced by the construction manager. So too would overall design and construction management developments both need to be reported to the client/client project manager for final decision-making. The organization therefore is one that naturally creates itself for each project by virtue of the discrete role and responsibility of each team member, almost regardless of the imposed method of procurement.

However, what is very different about the *temporary* construction project organization from the *permanent* organization is that the people filling the roles will be 'new' for each project, as will specialist trade contractors as they come and go over the course of a project. In other words the organization will, in part, have to be *established* at the inception of the project and continually *re-established* as it progresses. From another viewpoint, a construction project organization has to be continually *re-engineered* throughout the life of the project.

The *permanent* organization also has a reasonably well-established set of working procedures for its own corporately understood key processes, especially if it has developed a formal quality management system. The equivalent in the *temporary* construction project organization is the generic conventions of how one team member works with another. For example, the *designers* always produce design 'drawings and specifications' from which *construction managers* produce construction 'plans and programmes' — formerly by manual graphic and text methods but increasingly by electronic data methods through computer applications. Design change during construction is controlled by 'variation orders', 'architect's instructions', etc. However, beyond these very general conventions and other contractual 'procedures', there is no generally accepted formal method whereby the more detailed procedures of working together are defined. These tend to develop *ad hoc* for each project as it gradually evolves, and in one sense are naturalistic and happen as the need arises.

The problems that do arise constantly in a construction project between team members, however, often arise because of unclear detailed roles, relationships and procedures or untimely exchange of information between the designer, construction manager and specialist trade contractor.

Combining these two causes of problems suggests that it is the unfamiliarity of each 'team member' — both firms and people — with the working practices of the other that is the major disadvantage of the project's temporary organization over the permanent organization. Despite the generic conventions and contracts that the industry uses on every project, which everyone is familiar with through their ongoing professional practice, it is with the project-specific detail in terms of roles and information exchange where miscommunication occurs.

So, then, *unfamiliarity* with the *specific* needs of each new 'customer' and with the *specific* working practices of new 'team members' — as well as a lack of 'collective' *philosophy* towards the project — is the major disadvantage of the construction project temporary organization. Time at the beginning seldom allows for any period of familiarity before each new 'team member' firm or person joining has to immediately get on with their own particular role in the project. Any formal sort of 'organization' tends to be something that *evolves* as the project progresses rather than something that is *established* at its inception.

WHY DO PARTICIPATING FIRMS FAIL AS EFFECTIVE 'TEAM MEMBERS' IN PROJECTS?

As previously described, the 'team' as a whole and its 'members' as individual parts of that whole, as participating firms, happen as the project happens. *Specific* requirements and *unique* arrangements that become *known* or certainly become *clearer* as they progress are essential features of any construction project. This means that each firm that participates in the project, unless it is continually involved from inception to completion, tends to join a 'team' that already exists and is already working together. This being the case, it will either become — or *not* become — an effective 'team member' on the project depending on the manner of its 'joining'. The reasons why firms might *not* become or remain effective 'team members' could any of or any combination of the following:

- the cost, time and performance 'terms' on which they joined start to seem to be unreasonable or even unfair
- they are not made to feel part of the 'team' and courses of actions are being — or have already been — decided which could adversely affect them but for which they have had no part in making the decisions
- other projects with which they are becoming involved are starting to take priority over this one.

A major impact on each firm's effectiveness as a 'team member' will be how what it has to do is affected by what another 'team member' does — or does not do — either well or on time. If a specialist trade contractor does not have its contribution to the project managed well by the construction manager then it will probably be that it is the specialist trade contractor firm that appears ineffective! Equally, if the client project manager does not accurately convey the wishes of the commissioning client to either the construction manager or the designer they may not appear to be performing effectively.

WHO IS FAILING AND WHO IS SUCCEEDING IN 'ORGANIZATIONAL' TERMS ON PROJECTS?

It can be seen that one of the inherent problems of the temporary nature of a construction project's organization is that some team member firms are fully involved for most of the time but others will only be involved for part of the time. This will inevitably mean that those who join later will have to subscribe to an 'organization' which they have had no part in establishing. Although this is the normal way in construction, this situation may lead to the late-joining firms not being fully appreciative of the impact of early decision-making about the project, in which they took no part, but which may ultimately affect the roles and resources they need to contribute to play their part as an effective 'team member' firm.

Not being fully appreciative of their explicit (but also implicit) roles and resources requirements in the project's 'organization' means they cannot make their full contribution. If firms or individuals do not *know* what is expected of them then it is unlikely that they will *provide* what is expected of them! They will then be perceived to be *failing* the 'temporary' organization by the other 'team member' firms by default. The two ways in which any firm can be perceived to be failing the 'organization', and why, is as follows:

- a 'team member' firm can be perceived to be failing the construction project 'organization' if its *personnel* do not have a clear and meaningful organizational role in the project
- a 'team member' firm can be perceived to be failing in the construction project 'organization' if it is not providing enough *organizational resources* in terms of costs, time and quality needed for its particular contribution.

These perceptions of failure by other 'team members' and eventually by the firm and its personnel themselves can be:

- *demoralizing*, which inevitably leads to a reduction in *personal performance* by the firm's personnel involved
- *financially unrewarding*, which inevitably leads to a reduction in *business performance* for the firm itself.

These two outcomes feed upon themselves, causing a downward spiral which can end up as being a loss of both profit and reputation for the firm involved for having being part of the project's 'temporary' organization. Such a failure on one project for a firm will also damage its chances of succeeding on other projects as it has not had the 'experience' of success in order to repeat it in another project context.

All the above can happen to the firms and people of a client's project manager (and the client itself if the project manager is in-house), designer, construction manager or specialist trade contractor. Pure function does not exclude the possibility! And all firms of any type or size have probably had this experience of failure, and not success, as part of a project 'organization' at one time or another.

If it can be accepted that *any* firm intending to take part in a project must logically be doing so with the express purpose that it will benefit in business terms — both financially and for its reputation — it must logically follow that *no* firm wishes to fail as part of the project's 'temporary' organization. Therefore removing the causes of failure in the project process must be the approach to success for every firm involved. Turning potential 'losers' into certain 'winners' as 'team member' firms in the 'temporary' project organization must be fundamental to creating and sustaining the project team.

In broad terms, carrying out *any* project requires the organization of *people* and *resources* in such a way that the project objectives are realized. A construction project's organization is no different — despite its 'temporary' nature. Relating *people to people, people to resources,* and *resources to resources* appropriately is what needs to be 'organized' (Klean and Ludin, 1997). So therefore the 'wrong' people with 'unclear' roles and 'undetermined' relationships between them, coupled with 'insufficient' resources, is the ideal recipe for at least some — if not all — 'team member' firms and their people to fail!

The firm that will therefore most likely succeed as part of the project organization is one that will be selected on the basis of its:

- available people with skills and knowledge appropriate to the particular type of project
- available resources of time, money and quality standards to complete the particular size and complexity of the project.

However, the firm's success is also dependent on the above being available from all other firms involved in the project to which they have to relate their particular work. Finally, the overall project itself will be considered a success if it is so organized that at the very least, and as a whole, it:

- finishes on schedule
- finishes within the project budget
- meets all core objectives
- meets all stakeholders' expectations.

It is also suggested that a project can be perceived to be a success even if it does not achieve the first two of the above and considered a failure even if it does. Measured objectively, it would appear that, at the very most, success is perceived to be achieved in a project if:

- project objectives are achieved (which ideally include *time* and *cost*)
- all stakeholder expectations are met
- all the project team's expectations are met.

'A high level of satisfaction among everyone involved with the project and all those affected by the outcomes is perceived a measure of *success*' (Young, 1995).

It would appear to follow that the same criteria of success for the project as a whole apply to individual 'team member' firms. It could be argued that a project which, through its 'organization', came in under cost and time but financially ruined one or more 'team member' firms is not a success — and would certainly be considered a failure by the firms concerned!

Whether an individual firm succeeds or fails as part of the project's 'temporary' organization will therefore depend on:

- whether it is the 'right' project for it in terms of client, type, size and complexity, having regard to its own available people and resources
- whether the project management 'organization' as determined by the client or the client's project manager ensures the firm's individual contribution can be appropriately made in terms of time and its relationship to the contributions of other team member firms
- whether what has been 'promised' in the beginning by the individual firm and project management organization can be actually 'maintained and delivered' as the project progresses through its life cycle.

Any or all of the above criteria not being met will cause failure for someone.

WHEN DO THE 'ORGANIZATIONAL' PROBLEMS START IN THE PROJECT LIFE CYCLE?

Given that all team member firms start off with the intention of succeeding in the project, 'problems' must inevitably arise that divert them from this aim. Leaving aside the possibility that any one firm might be seriously affected in its performance and financial viability because of a problem in *another* project, what are the problems and when do they start for the project being considered? It can be generally observed from practice that when things go wrong during the course of a construction project their root cause can be traced to either:

- when the project was *first* initiated by the client or
- *when the particular firm through which or for which things have gone wrong was first* appointed.

More often than not, the 'problem' is about an unfulfilled 'expectation' by one party of another involved in the project process. For example:

- for the client, the overall cost and time are exceeding those which were promised at the beginning because the design and construction are taking longer than originally planned

- for a firm of specialist contractors, more work is entailed than that which the firm originally priced for in its accepted tender and for which the client is not willing to pay
- for the designer, a specialist contractor is not producing an elemental part of the building according to the aesthetic or functional standard envisaged in the design.

Change, of whatever sort and for whatever reason, from what was *first expected* by any team member firm involved becomes the basis of a 'problem', which can evolve into a 'dispute', which in turn usually has some sort of 'financial claim' — which gets resisted — as its ultimate outcome. Dispute *resolution,* by one means or another, has become a regular feature of the usual construction project process and in the end costs 'team member' firms money that can seriously affect their out-turn profit for the project if they are unsuccessful.

Dispute *avoidance* is therefore the hope of all project teams, both as individuals and business firms, and this can only happen by having the cause of potential 'problems' eliminated at their source. Given that the *individuals* involved have no vested interest in causing any 'problems' that might arise during the course of the project, it is most likely that these 'problems' are *organizational* ones. The 'problems' themselves nearly always focus on a lack of clarity about some aspect of the project information, for example:

- the original brief is 'unclear' about the detail and extent of all the client's project requirements
- the design drawings and specification are 'unclear' about the detail and extent of the designer's construction requirements for a specialist contractor's element
- the time and costs are 'unclear' about what exactly the values stated allowed for
- the responsibilities of individual team members in relationship to their duty towards others are 'unclear'.

Construction project management 'problems' probably all derive from the fact that there are unfulfilled expectations of one participant by another. This in turn can usually be traced to a lack of clarity in communication between the various participants because assumptions have been made which were incorrect. That is to say the other participant did not actually realize what was expected of it because of unfamiliarity with the normal working practices of the other participants.

WHERE ARE THE PROJECT'S 'ORGANIZATIONAL' OBJECTIVES SET?

In the manufacturing industries, or in any commercial organization, a 'project' becomes defined in order to meet some identified business strategy requirement, for example the need to create a new product or service — or revamp existing ones — in order to meet a future business financial aim. The reason for this 'project' is therefore reasonably well understood by all the people taking part within that organization once they have been appointed. So the *objectives* of the 'project' are known and shared by the essential participants, who all work for the same industrial or commercial organization right from the beginning.

'Where' they are set is therefore *in* the product or service organization which is the normal workplace for all the project participants. Even if outside agents are used, the focus of the project and its objectives is the business organization for which it has been set up in order to serve a specific purpose.

In construction, the business organization for which the project has been set up can only be that of the client. It is the client, and the client alone, who understands initially why there is a need for a new or rehabilitated building or civil engineering project. Depending on the client's situation, the project may have some social, political or environmental 'symbolic' significance over and above the creation of the facility itself.

Regardless of the particular project situation, the *project objectives* in construction are defined by the client and emanate from the client's business organization. Only the client can define these objectives, and, therefore, in order to ensure that they are clearly communicated, targeted, maintained and finally achieved throughout the project life cycle, the client needs to ensure that:

- the appointed project team is sympathetic to the objectives
- the project team has the skills, knowledge and resources as individual design and construction firms to achieve the objectives in practice
- the project team becomes, in effect, part of the client's organization and the expert 'agents' by which that organization realizes its objectives for the project.

Matching the organization to the *project objectives* then becomes the basis by which the *organization objectives* can be determined. However, it needs to be borne in mind that this 'organization' can only be a temporary one in business terms and needs to be rapidly formed as a cohesive entity as soon as each new participating firm joins the project. One problem that has to be addressed, therefore, is how *organization* objectives — that ideally need the sympathy and cooperation of all project participants who are to be 'organized' — can be effectively set when the main bulk of the participating construction firms — i.e. the specialist designers and contractors — are not yet appointed.

It would therefore seem to be that whilst *project objectives* need to be set and held firm, the *organization objectives* need to have some flexibility according to how and when each new participant is appointed to the project. That is, if they are to have the full sympathy and cooperation of each project participant. Forcing a specialist contractor firm that has been appointed on the basis of a lowest tender to participate in an organization arrangement that has not recognized that a particular firm's strengths and weaknesses is a recipe for disaster — and also the cause of demoralization, defects and claims!

Therefore, although like the project objectives, the organization objectives will be set initially in the client's organization, they must invariably vary to suit the changing project situation whilst always ensuring that the project objectives are being met.

HOW CAN THE INDIVIDUAL FIRM'S 'ORGANIZATIONAL' OBJECTIVES BE HARMONIZED TO MEET BOTH ITS AND CLIENT'S 'ORGANIZATIONAL' OBJECTIVES FOR THE PROJECT?

In a construction project, where the team comprises people from many different participating design and construction firms, it is inevitable that two sets of varying *business* objectives have to be catered for effectively if the project is to go well.

In the first instance, the client has *project* objectives which stem from the client's organization's *business* objectives and for which *project organization* objectives must be appropriate. In the second instance, each participating firm has its own ongoing *business* objectives, and *organization* objectives to suit. However, participating firms such as architects, engineers and construction managers are organized in a way that usually allows them to fit into a project organization. That is because their business is *projects* and their key people only serve projects as project architects, project engineers, *project* construction managers, etc. Moreover, these people are used to fitting into the 'temporary' organization of a project (in fact those of a number of different projects simultaneously!) and working with other people from other firms, as this is their normal method of working and they do it all the time.

In contrast, the client firm is probably organized to deliver whatever is the aim of its business in terms of a product or a service — for example a particular manufactured product or a health service — and this is not necessarily *project orientated* in the sense that the thing being delivered can be seen to have 'a beginning and an end' — it is, rather, 'continuously ongoing'. Although some of these firms will from time have their own internal projects — for example creating a new product or service line — their people are more used to working with other people *within the same firm*. The exception being where large client organizations are 'repeat-order' construction clients and have their own in-house *project* department — which usually comprises ex-construction professionals who are people used to working in temporary project organizations with people from other firms.

Therefore, with regard to differing organization objectives, the situation is that:

- client firms generally have organizations designed to support their people to deliver an 'ongoing service or product'
- design and construction firms have organizations designed to support their people delivering multiple 'projects' simultaneously to a number of different clients.

In other words, the design and construction firms have people continually organized to work on projects, whilst the client firms have people continually organized but not necessarily to work on projects. For each client's individual project the organization objectives must therefore be to:

- get the people from the client firm who need to be involved in the project in one way or another to fit into a temporary project organization (which it must support in achieving the client's project objectives)
- get the people from the design and construction firms to fit into the temporary project organization (as and when they are appointed over the life cycle of the project).

However, in getting its people to make these organizational adjustments, each firm must still hold to its own ongoing business objectives. The client must still ensure the project meets its defined cost, time and quality requirements and the design and construction firms must ensure that taking part in the project makes them a profit and enhances their reputation.

Therefore the temporary project organization objectives must comprise a judicious mix of each participating firm's individual business objectives if the resulting organization is to support all the people working together as a harmonious team. No-one must feel that their own firm's individual business objectives are being compromised, otherwise they will forced to take a defensive position to the detriment of the project as a whole.

WHAT ARE THE 'ORGANIZATIONAL' IMPLICATIONS OF THE INDIVIDUAL FIRMS COMBINING TO MAKE ONE TEMPORARY 'ORGANIZATION'?

It would seem that one of the strengths of the construction industry and its design and construction firms is the ability to adapt *organizationally* to whatever is required in terms of a client's project size or complexity. Its ability to form — usually at very short notice — and work within — very often for long times — temporary project organizations is innate and taken for granted as that is the only way the construction industry can work — despite various challenges from others to do otherwise! As stated previously, its design and construction firms are in fact organized as businesses to operate in this way, with people allocated to projects which become their own 'cost centres' needing to show the firm a profit as an one-off activity.

The weakness of the construction industry is that it is most likely that each temporary project is a unique combination of firms and people who have never worked together before and are not likely to work together again in the future. This has always meant that each time there has to be 'a learning curve' when each participant — both firm and people — gets to know how each other works to form an effective project team. Unfamiliarity with the others' philosophies and methods can often lead to the miscommunication which is usually the root cause of all disputes and claims that traditional JCT contracts have been developed to cope with and which have created the industry's traditional 'adversarial contractual' culture and practice environment. The concept of partnering (Bennett and Jayes, 1995) has obviously been developed to try and establish a culture of more long-term relationships to overcome this weakness of 'temporariness', but will only be appropriate in certain circumstances, for example where a client has a long-term construction programme.

The following key *organizational* criteria can be defined for all client, design and construction firms where they normally need to form a combined temporary project organization:

- each firm's existing organization has to adapt to a *unique temporary organization*
- each firm's existing organization has to adapt *immediately it is appointed*
- each firm's existing organization often has to adapt to *temporary organization that already exists* when, by reason of the contribution it makes, it is appointed later in the project life cycle.

So, whilst maintaining an organization that meets its own firm's ongoing business need, each firm's organization must be able to satisfy the above criteria. Satisfying these criteria would seem to suggest that it would be helpful if all design and construction firms:

- kept records of *project organizations and their implications* of past projects they have participated in so that the lessons from similar projects (the similarity being, for example, in type of facility, type of site or type of procurement method) can be rapidly learned and catered for in joining a current project
- developed a set of criteria that it expects to be met by the temporary project organization it is to join that will suit its own organization that has been developed to meet its own ongoing business needs.

Therefore the inherent adaptability of all design and construction firms' organizations to adapt to meet the temporary project organizations required by their clients needs to be *strengthened and systematized* if a successful combination is to be achieved for every person and the firm they represent in the project team.

WHO DIRECTS AND MANAGES THIS TEMPORARY 'ORGANIZED' TEAM OF FIRMS?

A construction project requires a temporary organization the mission of which is to meet the client's business objectives. Whether that 'organsiation' requires a leader and who that leader should be is a question of debate that still continues. To map the construction project 'organization' on to any other 'organization' means that there should be a clear leadership role. In permanent organizations the person who is the leader, who has the vision, who sets overall standards and who has overall authority, responsibility and liablity may be the chief executive, director, principal, etc., depending on the nature of that organization and the product or service it delivers.

In the temporary 'organization' of the construction project, what that leadership role is and who should fulfil it are not quite so obvious. For example the 'organization' in one sense is a coalition of different firms who all have a common objective to fulfil by each firm playing its distinct part. Traditionally — whether recently or historically — that leader has been someone called the 'architect' and the derivation of the name implies that he or she was the person responsible for the design and construction management of the whole process. Even though more recently the architect's role (for building projects) and the engineer's role (for engineering projects) has been reduced to that of overall designer and contract administrator, the architect was considered as the leader of the construction project. However, currently, the project leader, through the use of different methods of procurement, could be considered to be either the client (or its appointed project manager) or, conversely, the contractor when a whole package deal is offered. Others would argue (Gray *et al.*, 1994) that the leadership role can change according to the particular stage that the project is passing through. For example, the designer in the design stage, the contractor/construction manager in the construction stage.

The clear emergence of a role of *project manager*, particularly in building, might, however, mean that this discipline now constitutes the leader and overall manager of the project's temporary organization. Certainly in the New Engineering Contract (Insitute of Civil Engineers, 1998) the role of project manager is considered as one and the same as the *contract administrator* for the construction process. It also might be inferred from both the title and the defined responsibilities of the *project manager* that this is this person who should head up the tempo-rary project 'organization', in other words, be its chief executive, director, principal, etc. Or does the 'temporary and fluid' nature of the project organization, and its need for flexibility as the project proceeds, mean that no such equivalent *permanent* role is appropriate?

However, when a 'project' is created within a company for a specific purpose in the company's business development, the role of a clear project leader is recommended (Young, 1995) and is one without which the project cannot really succeed, even though that project leader is ultimately responsible to a project director for the duration of the project he or she is in charge of! Presumably, by definition, he or she is also the leader of the 'temporary' organization set up within the company to fulfil the objectives of the project. Harmonizing that 'temporary' organization with the 'permanent' organization of the company is an important part of the project leader's responsibilities. A similar 'harmonizing' requirement exists for the *construction* project's 'temporary' organization in relation to the 'permanent' organizations of the participating client, design and construction firms.

So the requirement for a clear direction through leadership and management for the temporary 'project' organization stems from the facts that:

- any organization, whether 'temporary' or 'permanent', needs a personal 'leader' who can provide vision and take overall responsibility and liability
- the harmonization of the 'temporary' project organization with the 'permanent' organization of the participating firms needs to be carried out with an overview of both types of organizations' objectives.

The question then remains as to who should fulfil that role. Out of the four key *functional* participants identified in a construction project – the client, the designer, the construction manager and the specialist trade contractor – in *functional* terms it would appear that the client is the best one to fulfil that leadership role. The logic of this stems from the fact that the client must take the leadership role as the ultimate decision-maker and anyway it is after all the client's project and nobody else's! Without the client the project would not exist. Where the client may not have sufficient 'in-house' skills to fulfil that role an externally appointed project manager, who can act solely on the client's behalf, can.

The client's project manager, whether 'in-house' or externally appointed, is the person to take the role of directing and managing the temporary 'organization', the sole purpose of which is to fulfil the client's project objectives. Indeed, as the function of *designing* and *constructing* is the function of the other participants, this would seem to be the *only* role for the client's project manager to fulfil. However, the role is an onerous one in that the team members, as both people and firms, are still very separate individuals employed by very diverse corporate entities that still have their own business interests to safeguard and professional interest to pursue as well as fulfilling collectively the project objectives.

Construction project managers face a greater challenge than project managers directing a project within their own company, because in terms of people management they can *only* rely on means *other* than command authority to get project objectives met (Beard, 1995). They must not only have a very clear vision of the business objectives of the client but also be appreciative of those of the participating design and construction firms in order to ensure that all team members are happy with their involvement and continue to make a positive contribution throughout the project's life cycle.

WHEN IS THE 'ORGANIZATIONAL' STRATEGY SET FOR THE PROJECT TEAM?

Any organization set up for any purpose needs to begin with an overall strategy. The purpose of a strategy is to be able to define an overview of the whole project before getting 'bogged down' in any detail. The value of this is to ensure that none of the critical factors that will affect the efficient and effective running of the project in order to meet its objectives are overlooked. If they are overlooked and 'emerge' unexpectedly during the project life cycle they can cause disruption, delay and demoralization, usually because work that has been done — especially in the design stage — needs to be redone. Rework, because new requirements have not been met, ultimately causes loss of profit to the participating design and construction firms because their 'costs' are increasing unexpectedly. Which in turn affects their business!

An *organizational* strategy for the project team should take account of the following factors:

* who all the 'stakeholders' are that have interests in the project — especially those who are not obviously part of the commissioning client's organization — and how they should fit into the 'temporary' organization depending on the strength of their impact on the project
* what the essential project objectives really are — which may be more than what is contained in the client's formal brief — and might be considered in terms of any 'hidden agenda' items
* how the project objectives can be met in terms of the involvement of appropriate design and construction firms — and other 'specialists' — over the life cycle of the project

- when key dates of critical events occur in the project life cycle, which can equally well be concerned with community as with client factors.

The project's 'temporary' organization should have the above strategic basis for its outline integrated arrangement of firms of people, as well as the process and programme by which they will work together throughout the project's life cycle.

It follows that *when* the strategy should be set must be *at the very inception* of the project and therefore it can only be set by the client's 'in-house' or externally appointed project manager, because this organizational strategy will determine:

- when all the other design and construction firms should be appointed
- how the organization should be developed as a process and programme
- what needs to be done, in what priority order
- who are the people who should be involved in establishing and running the organization.

However, given the reality of projects and that, usually because of unforeseen external circumstances, *change* would always seem to be inevitable, the organization strategy itself must recognize that possibility and always be capable of a degree of adaptation as the project progresses over its life cycle. It also needs to recognize the fact that unlike 'in-house' company projects, there is going to be a far greater chance of organizational change because of the multiplicity of different companies involved.

For example, in an 'in-house' company project there is alway the risk of a key person leaving the company for another post. In a construction project that risk is increased because a number of key people could leave each of a number of companies for another post. Althought the project manager may have some control in keeping a key person in an 'in-house' company project, he or she will have none over those who are involved in the project but work for other companies.

WHERE DO PROJECT TEAM MEMBERS MEET TO AGREE THE 'ORGANIZATIONAL' TACTICS?

It can be seen so far that the *members* of the team will comprise:

- different design and construction — and other specialist — business firms
- different *people* who work for those firms.

It is also obvious that not all the *firms* — and therefore their *people* — will necessarily be involved in the project right from the project's inception. Indeed some of the specialist contracting construction firms — as perhaps some of the specialist designers — might not become involved until the project is well under way and, depending on the skill they contribute, nearly finished. This means that these firms cannot be involved in forming the project's organizational strategy and tactics, as they are not around at the appropriate time. In fact, part of a project's organizational 'tactics' may well include how these specialist firms that are only needed later on will be actually appointed. How and when they are appointed — and the contractual conditions under which they are engaged — will affect the way they perceive themselves and are perceived by others as 'team members'. If other firms that have been appointed earlier have been engaged through *partnering* or *negotiated* arrangements and the later ones through *price competition*, the way they are regarded as part of the project 'organization' is likely to be different. The firms appointed earlier, and their people, may be regarded, and consequently feel, as 'insiders' while the firms appointed later, and their people, may feel like 'outsiders.' So, not only will a strategy and tactics have been decided upon to which these firms were not party but also the very strategy and tactics themselves have put these team-member firms at a *business* disadvantage to the others.

Any *un*equal membership of a team may result in resentment if that inequality is felt by the people of the participating firm so appointed. The organizational tactics formulated by the early team-member firms and their people, directed by the client's project manager, will be done by key meetings in the very early stages. On the basis of broad strategic objectives, specific methods of appointment and contractual conditions to meet key time objectives will be agreed by them at that time. For very practical reasons it will probably not be possible to involve the firms to be appointed in the *future* at that current time. However, the other *strategic* issues considered in the early phases, such as

- how the organization should be developed as a process and programme
- what needs to be done, in what priority order
- who are the people who should be involved in establishing and running the organization,

can all be developed as *specific tactics* for the temporary organization as and when each participating firm becomes involved. In fact, even if the firm is appointed on price competition, there is no disadvantage and every advantage in making the three types of specific requirements part of the specification/tender agreement. Giving a potential participating firm the assurance that it will be positively involved in the project organization *before* it tenders may even have a benefit for prices as it may feel that its own business interests will be well protected if it is appointed. There is in fact no reason why any potential team-member firm cannot be briefed on the whole project strategy and be informed of the tactics developed so far before they are appointed by either partnering, negotiation or price competition.

There is therefore no good reason why organization *tactics* — coming from the original or modified *strategy* — cannot be agreed with any team-member firm as and when it becomes a project team members. From both a human point of view for the people involved and a business point of view for the firms they represent, this would support the a harmonious involvement of each participant in the project team. Leaving even one firm 'out' of this process, regardless of the size of contribution it makes — either by design or default — could have serious consequences for realizing all the project's objectives if the firm's exclusion results in resentment and low performance.

WHEN DOES EACH FIRM KNOW THAT THE OVERALL 'ORGANIZATION' FOR THE PROJECT AND ITS OWN 'ORGANIZATION' HAS SUCCEEDED?

'Success' in a construction project can be many-faceted. For the client, the fact that the resulting construction came in on time and to budget, looked and performed as the client had expected, and satisfied every other 'stakeholder' would mean that the project could be considered a success. For the project manager, achieving the above would also mean it had been a success in terms of enhancing his or her reputation. However, if this had been at the expense of his or her time costs being higher than anticipated and priced for, that 'success' might be tarnished in terms of the financial aspect of his or her business. The same situation of tarnished 'success' could also apply to every other design, construction and specialist firm that took part.

The purpose of the project 'organization' must be to ensure every participating firms involvement can be considered a 'success'. In simple terms this must mean that not only did the client have all its expectations fulfilled but that every participating firm enhanced its reputation and realized its expected profit because its expected costs were not exceeded. If the project's 'organization' cannot deliver this realization then it will have only succeeded in part. The usual cause of a participating firm that is competent in its own particular field not being able to do all expected of it for a quoted price is that what was really expected of it when it was appointed was not absolutely clear.

Unknown or unrealistic 'expectations' of one participant of another is probably at the root cause of all construction project time, cost and quality 'failures'. More often that not the blame for this 'failure' is put on the firm that did not meet these 'expectations' — and *not* on the firm that was supposed to convey them as part of its duties and responsibilities. However, the real cause of this 'failure' will always lie somewhere within the project's 'organization'. If the 'organization' is putting any particular participating firm at any particular time at a disadvantage in the following areas of

- *not* agreeing with it its requirements for its participation
- *not* providing it with critical information on time
- *not* making it aware of the responsibilities of other team members and key people with whom it should communicate that will affect its work
- *not* making appropriate timely payments for work done
- *not* informing it of change and especially the need for any 'expediting',

then the 'organization' of the project could be said to be 'failing'. Conversely, if the project 'organization' is doing just the opposite then it could be said to be 'succeeding' both for the overall project and the participating firm. In its turn each participating firm needs to have its own internal organization that matches the overall project 'organization' in order to have its own method of:

- agreeing its requirements
- identifying the need for and reception of timely critical information
- defining its own responsibilities and key people with whom other team members should communicate in order for it to carry out its work
- determining and applying for appropriate timely payments for work done
- coping with change and especially the need for any 'expediting'.

When both the overall project 'organization' — usually controlled by the client project manager — and the individual team-member firm's own internal matching 'organization' are working as described, then it could be said that both are 'succeeding'. A deficiency in any one particular area described above would mean that the 'organization' is 'failing'.

IN CONCLUSION

Construction project teams are unique in that:

- they are formed to create construction 'products' for very individual clients and can be considered to be 'one-off'
- they comprise a 'team' of separate design and construction firms that are diverse in nature but all have in common the 'business' of construction projects.

They are *not* unique, in that:

- they comprise different types of people from different types of design and production disciplines who have to come together to do their work in the realization of a construction project
- their essential purpose to fulfil a clearly defined project need by integrating the processes of design and production.

Their fundamental strengths are:

- the 'customer needs' they have to satisfy with their 'product' are very focused in a specific 'client's brief'
- they comprise people who are extremely adaptable and flexible in their method of working because of the 'uniqueness' of the projects on which they have to work
- they have inherent organizational capabilities that, through tradition, can cope extremely well with changing circumstances and adapt to new situations.

Their fundamental weaknesses are that:

- they comprise firms and people who may well have never worked together before in the past and are not necessarily likely to do so in the future, and consequently have to go through a communication 'learning curve' at the beginning of each new project

- they use working conventions that are not necessarily that precise or formal or appropriate to any particular project and are bound together with traditional 'adversarial' contracts.

Given the above analysis of construction project teams, they have to do the following in order to maximize their inherent strengths and minimize their inherent weaknesses:

- establish an agreed working-together method from project inception that all subsequently appointed participating firms will accept
- exploit their individual people's disciplines for the benefit of the client's project as well as each firm's own business success
- enhance the reputation of all participating firms through positive organization and leadership in order to get their full commitment towards each other and the project as a whole.

Finally, if construction project teams are to 'succeed' in fulfilling the client's aim for the project then each participating firm must also experience its participation as a 'business' success. The critical issues involved in ensuring the project organization successfully combines the diverse disciplines, stakeholders, people and businesses through effective information exchange are discussed in the subsequent chapters.

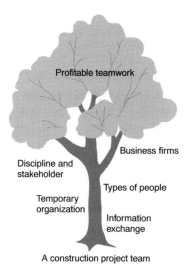

An integrated approach. Reconciling the diverse aspects of a construction project team to support profitable teamwork

4

A team of diverse people and cultures — dealing with the differences

INTRODUCTION

In Chapter 2, we suggested that any design or construction organization — regardless of size or type — can only carry out its day-to-day business by becoming involved, either sooner or later, in a construction project *team*. In Chapter 3 we suggested the generic composition of any construction project team — regardless of project size and complexity — that comprised not only the commissioning client and main design and construction disciplines, but also all the other stakeholders that would become directly or indirectly involved in the project.

In this chapter we consider the issues involved in effective *team-working* that arise because the team comprises diverse types of people with diverse cultural backgrounds. We also suggest that this diversity has a major impact right from the inception of the project. Unless this *human* aspect of people working together in teams is recognized right from the beginning of a construction project, diversity of personality type and cultural background may cause *personal* conflict that inhibits achieving the project's objectives.

HUMAN RELATIONSHIP THEORY — DIVERSE PEOPLE

In all human relationships and transactions there are 'expectations' on both sides. That those 'expectations' are, more often than not, either unrealistic or not understood probably lies at the root cause of unful-filled 'expectations'. What one person thought that the other person was 'promising' was not actually the fact — usually because the person offering did not actually know what the other actually 'expected'!

Misunderstood, and subsequently unfulfilled, 'expectations' by one person of another leads to:

- *personal* disappointment, a sense of being 'cheated' and in extreme cases of being 'betrayed' — especially where a given trust has not been respected
- a risk of future personal 'retaliation' in the relationship — either consciously or even subconsciously — causing the relationship to slowly but surely deteriorate.

If this happens in a construction project then the likely consequences are that:

- common objectives shared by all the participants at the beginning are no longer shared and consequently performance is reduced
- claims for *un*expected work different from that which was first tendered for and agreed are made, disputes are engendered and if unresolved may result in costly legal action.

Observed human relations in management studies indicate that people differ in a number of specific ways with regard to their resulting personal behaviours — especially in relationship to others in groups or teams. More often that not, it is the lack of understanding, recognition and respect for these differences that causes the miscommunication which results in unfulfilled 'expectations'.

Through a self-perception analysis (Belbin, 1997) individuals come up as different types with regard to the role that they can best, or worst, play in any team. The basis of the team role type definition is an inter-pretation of how individual people know they act themselves in a variety of group situations. The results of individual tests usually mean that the person recognizes him- or herself and the way he or she acts in group situations as either as 'plant', 'resource investigator', 'coordina-tor', 'shaper', 'monitor evaluator', 'teamworker', 'implementer' or 'completer'.

The purpose of this type of analysis is to show:

- the type of role that any individual can most naturally play, the ones that he or she can manage and the ones that, if possible, should be avoided

- the strengths and weaknesses of each role type
- the weaknesses that can be allowed by an individual person — and those that cannot — if the team is to work effectively.

Broadly speaking, the role types range across those who can generate ideas and 'spark' others, those who can coordinate, those who can research, monitor and evaluate and those who will work consistently to complete a task. The full set of team roles, their individual strengths and weaknesses, and allowable and not allowable weaknesses for effective teamworking are shown in Appendix 1. However, in an ideal world, the Belbin team role types means that for an effective project team there should be:

- a good balance of team role types represented across the key individuals who comprise the project team
- each team member understands the team role type of him- or herself and each other member and respects it
- team *leadership* uses the strengths of each role and makes allowances for certain weaknesses in each but not others.

Another, similar self-perception analysis test (the Myers–Briggs test — Oakland and Morris, 1997) defines individual people as specific combinations of personality types in terms of either being 'introvert' or 'extrovert'; 'sensing–thinking' or 'sensing–feeling'; 'intuition–thinking' or 'intuition–feeling'; and 'judging' or 'perceiver' types. The basic types and all possible type combinations are shown in Appendix 1. In human management theory, this is an alternative, but in some ways complementary, way to that of Belbin for defining the differences between people in groups. Again, in an ideal world, a construction project team should comprise a good balance of these type combinations, with mutual recognition and respect of each for the other.

In current management theory thinking, yet another approach has emerged of how people differ in their way of thinking and how this in turn affects how others can effectively communicate with them. Neuro-linguistic programming (NLP) (Bradbury, 1997) proposes that people fall into three different categories according to a 'preferred thing style' (PTS). These are *visual, auditory* and *kinetic,* and whichever category any one individual falls into as his or her strongest PTS can be reasonably deduced from the way he or she talks, looks and position him- or herself in any human transaction. Again, in an ideal world, a balance of people who see things in different ways might ensure that all-round view of a project is taken to make sure that nothing is missed.

As long as the different PTSs are recognized and respected in the team's communication process.

If the combined Belbin, Myers–Briggs and NLP analysis and categorization of people was used to first identify, and then provide ongoing support for, the 'ideal' team in human personality terms, personality clashes and miscommunication problems in construction project teams might be avoided.

However, as described in Chapter 3, construction project teams will be appointed primarily because of the particular discipline skill, expertise and experience that the individual company or company individual has to offer and the project needs by virtue of its specific social, political, economic and technical requirements. The reality is that because of the very nature of the construction project team – and very often the speed with which it has to be assembled – what must come first is the ability of team members, both firms and individuals, to be able to perform their *technical* contribution in an effective and economic manner. It would be very difficult for a project manager to convince a client that a particular firm and individuals who offered a competitive price and appropriate quality standard with their work should *not* be appointed because of the risk of a 'personality' clash with another team-member firm or individual!

What is required in construction project team leadership and management is therefore that, at the very least, there is:

- the recognition that these differences occur in the personalities and operating styles of every individual team member and that these differences will affect, positively or negatively, how people work both as individuals and together as a team
- the use of these different personality types and operating styles by encouraging individual team members to play their most natural role in order to create a dynamic yet balanced team through personal strengths as the project evolves
- the monitoring of these different personality types and operating styles in order to ensure that the personal weaknesses of individual team members do not adversely affect efficient and effective teamworking.

An awareness of these interpersonal factors in a construction project team right from the beginning is vital. The most expert technical contribution to a project team could be negated by a personal conflict. The clear, agreed social and economic objectives set by the early team members could be lost later in the project if later team members cause conflict in teamworking for personality reasons.

Even though pressure of time in a fast-moving project may seem to inhibit the necessary analysis and team training for each and every team member to become aware of the personality issues, *not* doing so could have much more ultimate negative cost and time consequences.

HUMAN RELATIONSHIP THEORY – DIVERSE CULTURES

A 'culture' could be defined as *a set of beliefs, values and behaviours owned and practised by any group of human beings* — regardless of the size, type and complexity of the group. A group 'culture' is something that becomes ingrained over time and is not necessarily that easy to define in precise terms. Members of the group are influenced by this 'culture' almost subconsciously and their practice of its implicit behaviours can become 'natural' through the desire to be part of a group identity. For an individual to break from the group culture can be extremely difficult and traumatic — for the group to change its inherently ingrained culture to any extent is almost impossible.

'Cultures' exist for families, tribes, ethnic groups, nations, organizations (whether they be political, religious, leisure, social, economic or business organizations) and even for any project, which very soon becomes a 'temporary' organization comprising a group of individuals at any one time in its evolution. Individual 'cultures' will also exist for the various professional disciplines, particular types of client and the various 'stakeholders' who become involved in a project — architects, construction managers, public or private clients, etc.

The major 'cultural' differences seen in Chapter 9 are between those of two different economies — the *existing* market economy of the West and the *emerging* market economy of an eastern European country coming from a command economy background. In the other case studies the 'cultural' diversity will be concerned with different 'professions' and types of client and stakeholders.

In any construction project team — if the *team* can be taken as not only the major disciplines but all the stakeholders in the project — there has to be not only a merging of diverse *personalities* but also of diverse *cultures*, in some form or another all the diverse types of 'culture' described above. Just as individual *personalities* have strengths and weaknesses for effective teamworking so too do individual *cultures*.

These cultures can therefore be ascribed to:

- distinct stakeholder, client, design, construction or specialist contractor *organizations* by virtue of their individual company nature
- distinct *construction disciplines* by virtue of them being architects, engineers, construction managers and specialist contractors' professions and trades
- distinct groups of people in any or either of the above groupings by virtue of their *national/economic* backgrounds.

How both these *people* and *cultural* differences can be coped with in order to support efficient and effective project teamworking is explained in the following section.

HUMAN RELATIONSHIP THEORY – BUILDING AND LEADING TEAMS

Perhaps the most difficult, yet most promoted, aspect of human relations in organizations is that of 'team-building' and 'leadership'. Although all organizations, whatever their business and whether they are 'temporary' for projects or 'permanent', need to address these common 'people' issues, the temporary 'organizations' of construction projects have their peculiarities.

The most important starting point in construction projects for the human aspect of building and leading the project team is that, as described before, all people are *different* in terms of their natural character, temperament, emotional response levels, beliefs, etc. — all of which have been affected over time by their own *different* experiences. If people are to be motivated and to work together in 'teams' then there may be aspects of the construction project that inhibit doing the things that allow this to happen. For example, it is suggested, for the *motivating* project team leader, that he or she should consider that, however different the team members are, they will have some things in common because of their basic human nature (Losoncy, 1997). These are that *it is only human nature*:

- to want to grow (actualize)
- to want to contribute
- to want to belong
- to be open to explore new ideas
- to have an individual view of situations (despite the facts).

And because all people have their *personal logic* about the world around them, they have their own 'insights' about all situations, which if ignored can *de*motivate them but if encouraged can motivate them. However, it might be the case in a construction project that, because of the procurement method, brief or design specification, some project team members might be inhibited in satisfying the above human 'wants'. The architect might or might not be *open to explore new ideas* depending on the constraints of the brief, as might the specialist trade contractor because of the constraints of a prescriptive design specification. Legal contracts might also severely restrict the application of any *individual's view of situations* as the project progresses. And so on.

Inspiring all project team members to perform to the best of their ability — and, even more important, inspiring them to *cooperate* as and when it is necessary — has to be a major key to success in the management of a construction project. With the rise of *project management* as both a discipline and a required service in construction, this task must fall to the appointed *project manager*, who should be the 'leader' of the overall team — and who may be 'in-house' from the client's own organization or externally appointed.

Given all the likely 'constraints' of a construction project, team-building and leadership are crucial and the impact of their successful application on restricting project cost growth in major projects has been demonstrated by applied 'benchmarking' research (European Construction Industry, 1998). It is most likely that out of the two, effective leadership is the more important in that it must come first before teams can be 'built'. 'Leadership' itself actually holds no mysteries and what good leaders do — those who might be considered as *natural born* leaders — can be learned and applied by anyone. At a fundamental level effective leadership can only be carried out through personal power and not command authority. this is especially true in construction project teams, where those who 'lead' do not actually 'employ' those they have to lead. It is also true than in a project team situation any individual will either be *positively for* the leader and other team members or *negatively against* them (Beard, 1996). It is also now fairly well known how teams come together over time and therefore how the people involved will behave and act towards each other over time (Oakland and Morris, 1997). Teams are considered to evolve through the following stages:

- *forming* — during which personal feelings are covered up, people conform to established lines, no account is taken of others' values and views and there is no shared understanding of the task

66

- *storming* — during which more risky, personal issues are opened up, the team becomes more inward-looking and there is more concern for the values and problems of others in the team
- *norming* — during which there is confidence, trust within the team, a more systematic approach, more value given to others and clarification of objectives, all options are considered, detailed plans are prepared and there is a progress review for improvement
- *performing* — during which there is flexibility, leadership is decided by the situation and not protocol, everyone's energies are utilized and the basic principles and the social aspect of the organization's decisions are considered.

The sooner any project team gets to the final stage the better. In *construction* projects there is the problem that in the early stages a 'team' of key participants may grow together and stay together to the end of the project, but then have others join them from time to time as new 'members' as the project progresses. The other feature of the construction project is that just when it has got to its most *performing* level, it is disbanded because the project has finished. The use of 'partnering' approaches, described elsewhere in this book, is currently being tried to overcome what might considered a waste of a valuable human resource — the high-performing team!

'Leadership' of teams in practice can also be said to go through stages as the leader gains more confidence in the team members gaining more confidence in each other. Leadership is considered to evolve through the following stages:

- *directing* — during which the 'leader' is very directive giving clear instructions to meet agreed goals
- *coaching* — during which the 'leader' adopts a more coaching approach as the team becomes more experienced
- *supporting* — during which the 'leader' gives some help allowing more initiative by members of the team
- *delegating* — during which the 'leader' is able to take a role as a team member because the team have developed as his or her 'followers'.

The relationship in the stage of development between 'team-building' and 'leadership' is such that as the team itself moves towards greater cohesion then 'leadership' can become much less dictatorial. It can also be that skilled leadership itself can move the 'team-building' through the four stages and get a performing team very quickly.

Although both the above concepts apply to project teams in general, again there are features of the *construction* project team that make their application very specific. For example, the often very fast pace at which a construction project starts up because of pressures from the client means that there is no other option for the key participants than to become a 'performing' team as fast as possible. Also 'leadership' — with or without an appointed project manager — may also be very loose as each participant gets on with his or her own particular contribution. Because design concepts usually have to be produced first before other work can be carried out there is a *de facto* 'discipline leadership' by the architect or engineer as a *design* member of the team. As stated in Chapter 3, construction project teams also have the characteristic that some participants are there all the time from inception to completion and others may only be involved for short periods as the project develops and becomes more and more finalized in physical construction terms — for example a finishing-trade specialist contractor. For the latter participants the opportunity to gain any sense of belonging or being able to contribute, or to explore new ideas may be very limited.

Given these natural constraints of a construction project, whoever is responsible for the 'leadership for team-building' needs to be very aware of the importance of:

- making the new participant members feel they belong and can make a significant and meaningful contribution that is recognized
- making them, consequently, 'performing' team members as soon as possible
- ensuring that leadership also moves to the 'delegation' model for them as soon as possible.

The penalty for not recognizing the *human* aspect of people participating in construction project teams through the application of leadership and team-building skills is all too obvious from the experience of practice. First there is personal *resentment* by the firm's project representative and then there is corporate *retaliation* by the firm itself through non-performance in terms of time, cost (by claiming 'extras') and quality (by skimping on standards) — which on being required to perform the work again only builds more resentment and causes further delay.

Finally, it is important to recognize that, human nature being what it is, differences between people will arise during the course of even the best organized and led construction project. For a start, all participants are specialists by their own discipline experience, be they concept architect or trade craftsman, and therefore have a particular 'view' of the project (see also Chapter 8). This 'professional' or 'trade' view will reinforce, as well as be reinforced by, their own personal view based on their individual characteristics and personal logic view of the situations in which they find themselves. A different view of any situation is likely to be interpreted as a 'personal' difference and the sooner it is resolved the better for the benefit of the project as a whole.

Resolving differences is probably the most important aspect to team-building and maintaining. Suggestions of how this is done (Losoncy, 1997) are that the team leader, whoever that may be at whatever stage of the project, needs to use, or encourage other team members to use, one or all of the following techniques:

- *transferring* — which is getting into another team member's shoes and trying to understand the situation from his or her unique perspective
- *undiagnosing* — which is getting rid of an immediate 'judgemental label' for a team member and coming up with a view of the problem from that team member's 'personal logic'
- *peeking* — which is looking behind a team member's surface behaviours and feelings and looking for his or her true motivations
- *de-escalating* — which is resisting the temptation to judge as the team member speaks, which might lead to conflict, and listen to understand his or her feelings about the situation
- *exposing* — which is revealing one's own pressures and demands so that other team members see things from that point of view
- *linking* — which is pointing out similarities between different team members to help them overcome their fear of surface differences.

All the above means that one person needs to see any situation that is creating differences from the other person's point of view. Although *legally and contractually* an 'independent' view taken in traditional contracts by the architect or currently by the project manager may help this to happen, there may be strong *professional and contractual* pressures for everyone concerned to 'stick to one's guns' — especially if the differences in views are due to an oversight by the architect or project manager! However, experience of practice shows all too often that if *personal differences* are not quickly resolved they very quickly escalate into *company disputes* between participating firms, the result of which becomes wasteful in both time and cost and may well end up in very expensive legal claims with one or more financial losers!

Finally, it is worth making the observation that the people who work on construction projects are for the most part extremely adept at being tolerant and willing to compromise with others during the course of a project. This because they *really have to* in order to fulfil the role and responsibilities. This is because fulfilling theirs is so highly dependent on other team members carrying out *their* roles and responsibilities. For example a *project manager* is solely dependent on *designers* and *construction managers* to deliver the client's project, the *designers* are dependent on the *construction managers* to make their design 'concepts' a 'physical reality', the *construction managers* are solely dependent on the *specialist trade contractors*, and each *specialist trade contractor* is dependent on the previous one for preparation and the following for looking after the specialist element they produce. Using the human relationship knowledge and skills described should add to those inherent 'people skills' that all construction disciplines seem to acquire by virtue of the work they continually carry out.

In terms of *human behaviour* and relationships with other *people* in the team the very fluid nature of any construction project might actually be an advantage. Although the fact that construction teams 'come and go' on a project by project basis might be seen as a *disadvantage* in terms of a continuity of people working together, it might actually be an *advantage* in that the people involved do not have to continue a relationship that over time might go sour! Providing *a positive attitude and atmosphere* have been created for the project that they join, the fact that they have not met the other team members before and are not guaranteed to ever meet them again might not be the disadvantage that it is so often made out to be.

IN CONCLUSION

People who comprise construction project teams are very *different* in that:

- they have unique personal characteristics that makes them most naturally play particular team roles in human terms
- they have unique personal temperaments which make them think and act towards other people in certain ways
- all of these *personal* characteristics may be reinforced in behavioural terms by their particular culture, be that national or discipline-based.

People who comprise construction project teams are very much *the same* in that:

- they share a common human nature that means everyone wishes to grow, contribute, belong and explore and have their own 'personal logic' with which they view the outside world.

The leadership they require to be an effective project team needs to:

- recognize all the specific human characteristics mentioned above in each team member and to use them positively
- realize that if any team member is not *for* the leader and the team he or she will be 'against' the leader
- move from a position of directing to delegating a soon as possible — and especially with regard to people joining the project in its later stages.

The generic process of forming and building a team means an effective project team needs to:

- move from a position of 'storming' to 'performing' as soon as possible — and especially with regard to people joining the project in its later stages.

The nature of construction projects means that:

- differences of view between people will always arise, which if not resolved will become disputes between the participating firms they represent.

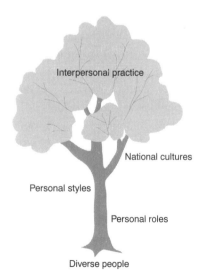

An integrated approach. Reconciling diverse personal styles, roles and cultures to support interpersonal practice

5

A team of diverse disciplines and stakeholders

INTRODUCTION

In Chapter 2, we suggested that any design or construction organization — regardless of size or type — can only carry out its day-to-day business by becoming involved, either sooner or later, in a construction project team. In Chapter 3 we suggested that the generic composition of any construction project team — regardless of project size and complexity — includes the commissioning client, the main design and construction disciplines and, if the wider team is considered, a considerable number of stakeholders who are either directly or indirectly involved in the project. In Chapter 4, the diverse types of people and cultures were considered and the ways of recognizing these differences in order to avoid 'personality and culture' clashes were suggested.

In this chapter we consider the issues involved in effective teamworking that arise because the team comprises diverse types of construction *disciplines* and — when the wider team is considered — other *stakeholders*. We suggest that this diversity also has a major impact right from the inception of the project. Unless this discipline and stakeholder diversity of people working together in teams is recognized and managed from project inception, diversity of discipline approach and stakeholder interest may cause conflict and inhibit the achievement of project objectives.

CONSTRUCTION MANAGEMENT THEORY – DIVERSE DISCIPLINES

The construction industry is multifaceted in its composition. In some ways it is hard to view it as a comprehensive, integrated industry at all. Its divisions into sectors and the fact that its commissioning clients – who range from public to private and from very small to very large organizations dealing with every social and technical aspect of a modern society – make it one that continually produces 'one-off' products. Its effort to 'standardize' technically is always thwarted because it has to respond to the needs of a very individual client for a very specific project.

This diversity of composition of the people and projects can be seen in each participant's own particular discipline interest in the project. To take an analogy from quality management systems thinking (British Standards Institution, 1997), the client can be seen as the 'customer' member of the team while the remaining design and construction disciplines can be seen as 'supplier' members in terms of the finished construction 'product'. The diversity of interest involved because of the different disciplines involved can be described as follows.

THE CLIENT AS THE 'CUSTOMER' TEAM MEMBER

The motivation for any client to commission a project in the first instance can vary considerably. On the one hand a project might be commissioned to produce a facility having a very specific technical and operating function to serve the client's business – and on the other hand and at the other extreme a project may be commissioned by a client to merely process money or to make some sort of social or political gesture. Clients that have a very specific technical/operating function as the outcome of the project in general terms – for example a particular building type – may still be very different because, although they appear to want a similar building type, the way they operate their own businesses may be very different.

The commissioning client is in most cases also an organization with many different personal, departmental, technical and economic interests in the project. Clients can also be 'knowledgeable' about projects because they frequently build or 'ignorant' because they only build once or twice. This can mean that as the leading team member their behaviour can vary widely from project to project or even on the same project because of different department interests from time to time. With regard to the types of client organization, it has been suggested (Green, 1996) that in the 1990s it is not that easy – or even useful – to specifically categorize clients from the briefing point of view. Clients can be viewed as *sophisticated* or *naive*; *primary* or *secondary* constructors, where the former build to get income and the latter build to provide a 'facility' for their ongoing business; *continuing* or *'one-off'*; *small* or *large*; *public* or *private*; *developer* or *owner occupier*.

However, in reality, these descriptions are too simplistic and mechanistic, and client organizations, because they comprise different people in social groupings, can only be viewed through a series of 'metaphors'. These 'metaphors' (Morgan, 1986), rather than providing convenient *categorization* of a particular client, provide a number of different *insights* in order to help to understand the nature of the client organization as part of the project team. The eight 'metaphors' proposed are:

(1) goal-seeking machines with interchangeable parts working in harmony to achieve a set of objectives and, in business terms, to maximize profits
(2) biological organizms that continually change to adapt to changing external environments
(3) organisms that possess a central 'brain' or intelligence that gathers information and dispenses instructions to the outlying 'limbs'
(4) cultural systems with shared values and beliefs
(5) political systems with individual and group power shifts and struggles
(6) psychic prisons in which people are trapped into a favoured way of thinking
(7) abstract transformations which are never really 'fixed' in time
(8) instruments of domination and the means by which individuals impose their will on others.

Understanding of the nature of the client organization *as an organization*, as soon as possible and as in as much detail as possible, by the other team members, is vital for effective teamworking. The nature of the client organization will tend to affect how the individual or group client 'representatives' behave as project team members. It should also be borne in mind that their power and influence on how the team can work will also be considerable as they are the team members for whom the whole purpose of the project exists and without whom there would be no project at all.

THE DESIGN AND CONSTRUCTION DISCIPLINES – THE 'SUPPLIER' MEMBERS OF THE TEAM

The responsibility for being an effective 'customer' member of the project team lies with the client; however, the responsibility for actually delivering the design and construction lies which the remaining 'supplier' team members. These 'supplier' team members are:

- architects and specialist engineers (structural, services, etc.), who are the 'consultant' *designers*
- main contractors or construction managers, who are the 'contractor' or 'consultant' *construction organizers*
- specialist trade 'direct contractors' or 'subcontractors', who the actual *constructors* of the elemental parts of any building or civil engineering facility to the client as the 'customer'.

Together, these disciplines and the various organizations that they operate from 'supply' the total facility which the project has been established to deliver

As 'organizations' it could be argued that each and every one of them could also be viewed in terms of Morgan's 'metaphors' just as for the clients. It would also follow that all of the disciplines' team members will be influenced in their behaviour by the 'organization' that they come from as much as they are influenced by the practice and values of their particular discipline. It may therefore be that, almost by accident, any construction project team may comprise a collection of organizations that do, or conversely do *not,* harmonize because of their underlying nature as organizations!

However, their traditions and professional experience as a *discipline* will strongly influence the way they perform as a project team member.

ARCHITECTS – THE CREATIVE 'WHOLE-BUILDING' CONCEPT DESIGNERS

All the 'designers' involved in the construction project team, including those from the specialist trade contractors, are 'creative' to some extent by virtue of their 'design' role. The architects in building design have a specific creative role in that:

- they conceive of the whole building form, fabric and structure as a perceived solution to the client's brief

- they therefore create the 'design framework' to which all the other subsequent designers have to relate
- they, more than any of the other subsequent designers, who focus on specific technical detail, take on in their thinking all the social and psychological aspects, as well as general technical aspects, of the project's 'end product' facility.

Many studies have been carried out over the past 20 years on the nature of the architectural design process — mainly for the purposes of seeing if it could be automated in computer-aided design (CAD). These studies (e.g. Broadbent, 1973; Paterson, 1980; Lawson, 1983) provided an insight into the architect's design process and method of thinking. Summations of that work for the purposes of quality management and computer integration studies (Cornick, 1991, 1996) suggest that the design process is one in which the architect goes through an implicit thinking cycle of analysis–synthesis–evaluation or conjecture–refutation.

During that process, the whole building design concepts that he or she generates through internal thought processes are being externally represented through manually or computer-generated graphical images. It is a process of rationalized thought which takes in all sorts of technical and aesthetic 'input information' on the basis of past experience and current fashion that might be appropriate to the given project brief in terms of its site location and type of facility. The architect has to eclectic in his or her thinking in arriving at possible solutions, which have to take account of such factors as:

- aesthetic and functional harmony with the project's physical environment
- aesthetic and functional requirement in the client's brief
- legislation concerning the facility use and site
- the nature of materials and systems for all the building elements
- the likely construction cost and time implications of the design proposals and how they meet the wider brief in general terms
- social and psychological factors that are pertinent to the project.

As a team member, the project architect — or design team leader, with large, complex projects — of the construction project team will therefore think and operate in the manner that best suits his or her chosen discipline — that is, to be a 'designer'. It is therefore natural for the architect, *as belonging to a particular discipline*, to think the most widely about the evolving project from a 'design' perspective. It is probably this ability to take such a 'holistic' view of the project that has put the architect in a natural position of team leadership historically.

If the project concerns a *building*, the architect needs to be understood by and behave appropriately towards the other team members so as to ensure that:

- his or her evolving 'holistic' design concept is appreciated by the client 'customer' team member as satisfying the project requirements
- the remaining 'supplier' team members can appreciate the construction cost, time, quality and safety implications of the evolving 'holistic' design concept.

ENGINEERS – THE SPECIALIST 'CONSTRUCTION ELEMENT' DESIGNER

In the majority of buildings, structural, services and particular specialist engineers are also 'designer' members of the project team. Each makes his or her own creative contribution to a specific aspect of the building's elements – e.g. structure, environmental systems and communications systems.

Tradition has it that the architect creates the overall building form, for which the engineers then design the various elemental parts to support that form structurally and environmentally. However, the complexity and performance demands of modern buildings mean that its various engineering elements require as much 'creativity' by the engineers in finding solutions for the structural and services elemental and system parts as is required by the architect for the whole building. The *structural* engineer therefore plays a very creative role in the concept design of modern buildings, where the structure becomes a very significant part of the *aesthetic,* as well as the *functional,* design (Addis, 1994). The same argument could be applied to the *civil* engineer where the construction is a civil engineering project such a road, bridge or dam, in which the 'structure' is essentially the construction's aesthetic as well as its functional design. With regard to the *services* or *environmental* engineer, the services have become a major element and system in most buildings. In quite a few notable ones with large open spaces and structures the services play a major – if not *the* major – part of the building's aesthetic as well as its functional design. In civil engineering process plant construction it could be argued that the services element *is* the total functional as well as the aesthetic design.

Although it can be argued that in modern building and civil engineering construction projects both architect *and* engineer play an equal 'creative' role as designers, as a discipline – and therefore as project team members – engineers can be *different* from architects. The engineer has to be focused in his or her thinking in arriving at possible structural or environmental services solutions, which have to take account of such factors as:

- aesthetic and functional harmony with the building's architectural design where the structure or environmental services are visually exposed
- functional requirements in the client's brief and those determined by the architectural design for the structural and environmental systems
- legislation concerning the structural and services elements
- lthe nature of the materials and systems for these specific elements
- the likely construction cost and time implications of these elements' design proposals and how they meet the wider brief in general terms.

As a team member, the project engineer – or design team leader, with large complex projects that are biased towards the engineering elements – of the construction project team will therefore think and operate in the manner that best suits his or her chosen discipline – that is, to be a 'designer'. It is therefore natural for the engineer, *as belonging to a particular discipline*, to think in a focused way about the evolving project from an 'elemental design' perspective – be that the structural or the environmental services. It is probably this ability to take such a 'holistic' view of the project that has put the architect in a natural position of team leadership historically.

If the project concerns a *building*, the engineer needs to be understood by and behave appropriately towards the other team members so as to ensure that:

- his or her evolving 'elemental' design concept is appreciated by the client 'customer' team member as satisfying the project requirements
- the remaining 'supplier' team members can appreciate the construction cost, time, quality and safety implications of the evolving 'elemental' design concept.

CONSTRUCTION MANAGERS – THE 'WHOLE-BUILDING' CONSTRUCTOR

Construction managers, whether they be commercial contractors or professional construction managers, usually have a background of being a construction contractor. The skills and knowledge they have acquired from their particular work discipline are:

- an ability to convert the presented drawings and specification of a proposed construction into a feasible physical construction work plan
- a generic understanding of how people, materials and plant can be organized to produce a building or civil engineering construction in parts, and as a whole of and on a site
- a generic understanding of real construction costs based on past project experience and current labour, material and plant prices
- the control of construction workers and coordination of specialist trade contractor firms who produce the elemental parts of the physical construction
- legal requirements for construction activity.

Perhaps the greatest influence on their thinking *as a discipline* has been generated by the 'traditional' form of procurement in which as contractors they have to *react* to what has mostly already been decided about the project. That is to say that the *design specification* solution to the project, which will determine what is needed for *production of the construction,* has already been decided *before* they join the project team. What has made their situation even worse from the point of view of being an equal team member is that, after what is often quite a short tender period, during which they are able to familiarize themselves with the design specification, they become *contractually bound* to construct the design specification to the cost and time they have quoted. It has long been recognized that the reaction to this somewhat unfair position has been the generation of 'adversarial' legal contracts. These on the one hand try to make it fairer for them when 'extras' are revealed as the project progresses, but on the other hand makes resistance to those claims possible so that the client is not disadvantaged.

The reaction to this in modern times has been for the construction disciplines to find ways of being at the inception of the project so they can influence the evolution of the design for production purposes. As described and discussed elsewhere in this book, methods of procurement such design/build, construction management and partnering are all developed means by which the 'contractor' as construction manager can be a project team member right from the inception of the project and before 'design' begins. The good practice of the construction management method stresses the importance of the construction manager having equal status to the designer.

As a team member, the project construction manager – whether a professional construction manager or traditional contractor – of the construction project team will therefore think and operate in the manner that best suits his or her chosen discipline – that is, to be a 'constructor'. It is therefore natural for the construction manager, *as belonging to a particular discipline*, to think the most widely about the evolving project from a 'whole construction production' perspective.

If the project concerns a *building*, the construction manager needs to be understood by and behave appropriately towards the other team members so as to ensure that:

- his or her evolving 'holistic' production concept is appreciated by the client 'customer' team member as satisfying the project requirements
- the remaining 'supplier' team members can appreciate the client requirement and design specification implications of the evolving 'holistic' production concept.

How the construction manager is positively incorporated into the team as a key team member *after* the designers have produced their work if traditional forms of procurement are used needs to be carefully considered. Not only will the major decisions have been made about the *design specification* – and therefore many *construction production* implications – but in terms of 'belonging', a core team of the client and designers will already exist into which the construction manager needs to be positively welcomed and encouraged to become part of the team.

SPECIALIST TRADE CONTRACTORS – THE 'SPECIALIST BUILDING ELEMENT' CONSTRUCTOR

Specialist trade contractors, whether acting as direct trade contractors under the construction management method or as subcontractors to the main contractor under all others, are the firms that specialize in the production of specific construction elements. They may also produce a considerable amount of detail design specification of the specific construction element. The skills and knowledge they have acquired from their particular work discipline are:

- an ability to convert presented scheme or detail drawings and a prescriptive or performance specification of a proposed specialist construction element into, if required, a detail design specification and a feasible physical construction work plan
- a generic understanding of how specialist tradesmen, materials and plant can be organized to produce a specialist construction element of a building or civil engineering work
- a generic understanding of real construction costs for a specialist construction element based on past project experience and current labour, material and plant prices
- the control of specialist tradesmen who produce a specific construction element
- legal requirements for specific construction element activity.

Just as with the construction manager, perhaps the greatest influence on their thinking *as a discipline* has been generated by the 'traditional' form of procurement in which as *subcontractors* they have to *react* to what has mostly already been decided about the project. All the same 'negative' effects that the traditional form of procurement has had on the construction manager as a *contractor* have been passed onto them as *subcontractors*. It is probably worse, as they usually have very little time to think about their contribution to the project during what is usually a short tender period for a specific building element. However, modern methods of procurement are allowing specialist trade contractors to be direct contractors to the client (Flanagan and Gray, 1989). This is especially so where they are concerned with a major construction element that needs integrated production design as the scheme design evolves. In these situations they become key 'team members' from the inception of the project.

As a team member, the specialist trade contractor — whether a sub- or direct contractor — of the construction project team will therefore think and operate in the manner that best suits his or her chosen discipline — that is, to be a 'specialist constructor'. It is therefore natural for the specialist trade contractor, *as belonging to a particular discipline*, to think in the most focused way about the evolving project from a 'specific construction element production' perspective.

If the project concerns a *building*, the specialist trade contractor needs to be understood by and behave appropriately towards the other team members so as to ensure that:

- his or her evolving 'specialist' production concept is appreciated by the client 'customer' team member as satisfying the project requirements
- the remaining 'supplier' team members can appreciate the client requirement, design specification and other 'specialist' element production implications of the evolving 'specialist' production concept.

How the specialist trade contractor is positively incorporated into the team as a key team member *after* the designers have produced their work if traditional forms of procurement are used needs to be carefully considered. Not only will the major decisions have been made about the *detail design specification* of a specific construction element but in terms of 'belonging', a core team of the client, designers and construction manager will already exist. In this situation, the specialist trade contractor needs to be positively welcomed and encouraged to become part of the team.

OTHER STAKEHOLDERS – DIRECTLY OR INDIRECTLY INVOLVED IN THE PROJECT

Having considered how the major 'customer' and 'supplier' participants in the project, that is to say the client, designers, construction manager and specialist trade contractor, may behave and should be treated as part of the project team, it is also necessary to consider the other 'stakeholders' involved in the project.

These can be divided into two categories: those who have a *direct* involvement in the project and those who have an *indirect* involvement in the project. Those stakeholders having a *direct* involvement in the project could be considered as:

- In relation to the client:
  - company board directors
  - funding organizations
  - particular end-users of the completed construction
- In relationship to the designers:
  - specialist system designers
- In relation to constructors:
  - specialist system constructors.

Those stakeholders having an *indirect* involvement in the project could be considered to be:

- local authority statutory bodies such as the planning authority
- the local community
- special-interest 'pressure' groups
- politicians
- adjoining site occupants.

How and when and for how long any of these stakeholders need to be part of the project team will depend on their interest and the circumstances of the project. It is most likely that those *directly* involved will have specific requirements that support the aims and objectives of the project. It is most likely that those *indirectly* involved will have restrictions they wish to impose which may, if not handled carefully, divert from the project's aims and objectives.

Involving each stakeholder at the right time, even those indirectly involved, and affording them all the leadership and support given to the key team members may have its reward in that:

- their views will be heard even though all their desires cannot be met
- those who might be 'against' the project might be won around to being 'for' it
- as 'honorary' team members they may also feel more like supporting the others in a positive way rather than putting negative restrictions on them.

The penalty for not doing this could be far-reaching and long-term and result in unexpected extra cost and time delay, which in turn may demoralize the key team members and reduce their performance and effectiveness.

IN CONCLUSION

The clients, design and construction disciplines and stakeholders who comprise construction project teams are very *different* in that:

- they have unique and often complex company culture characteristics that makes them behave in a particular way as a group (which can apply equally to the firms of designers and constructors as to the client)

- they have unique professional characteristics which make them think in either a holistic or focused, design or production way about the project and behave in a specific way towards other team members
- they have a discipline group history which has traditionally set them in particular roles and relationships (including the client, through traditional contractual arrangements).

The design and construction disciplines and stakeholders who comprise construction project teams are very much *the same* in that:

- they share common general experience of construction project activity and its implications and impact.

The leadership they require to be an effective project team needs to:

- recognize all the specific company-cultural and professional-discipline characteristics mentioned above in each team member and to use them positively.

The generic process of construction projects means that many team members will join in later stages and that:

- team members joining an already established team must be made to feel welcome and belong very quickly.

The nature of the wider impact of construction projects means that:

- all other stakeholders need to be considered and their views heard as part of the project team; if these are not taken into account they may result in time delays and extra costs.

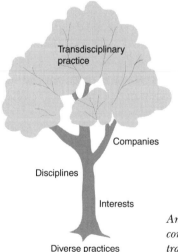

An integrated approach. Reconciling diverse companies, disciplines and interests to support transdisciplinary practice

6

A team of diverse businesses — meeting collective business objectives

Introduction

In Chapter 2, we suggested that any design or construction organization — regardless of size or type — can only carry out its day-to-day business by becoming involved, either sooner or later, in a construction project *team*. It will need to seek out client organizations that will have a definite 'business case' for carrying out a particular project. In Chapter 3 we suggested the generic composition of any construction project team — regardless of project size and complexity — which comprised not only the commissioning client and main design and construction disciplines, but also all the other stakeholders that would become directly or indirectly involved in the project. In Chapters 4 and 5 we suggested that the diversity of people, cultures, disciplines and stakeholders all need to be considered and dealt with in order to create a cohesive, performing construction project team.

In this chapter we consider the issues involved in effective team-working that arise because the team comprises diverse types of businesses, all of which have their individual business aims. As suggested in Chapter 2, although the client has a clear business aim in starting the project, so too must all the other participating firms taking part. The most difficult thing to ensure in a construction project in terms of business aims is making sure that every organization's aims are *collectively* met by *taking part together* in the project.

THE 'BOTTOM LINE' FOR EVERY FIRM

All businesses need to 'make money' — that is to say a profit, or if they are 'non-profit-making' organizations, a surplus. Unless what they receive exceeds their costs they will gradually go out of business through bankruptcy. Profit to satisfy shareholders, or surplus to satisfy trustees, is also the means by which any organization can find the money to invest for improvement in its ongoing business. Each business firm involved in the construction project has the aim that the outcome of the project will be a business improvement — and certainly *not* a business decline.

With regard to the client, this means that the final price of obtaining the project, any disruption caused by the actual work and the operating of the end-result facility will fit their intended business aims for having the project in the first place. If, through one reason or another, the final facility has cost too much, is too expensive to run or does not perform as expected in terms of an enhanced or expanded business operation — then the client's business aim will have failed to be achieved. Further 'projects' — which might not even involve construction — might then be needed, with their obvious further costs, to retrieve the business situation.

With regard to the other 'supplier' member business firms, this means at the very least that they do not want to lose money for having taken part in the project — and they will have preferably made the profit that they first intended when they tendered for the work and their price or fee was accepted. They also need to have performed how they promised, as the secondary 'business' aim they have for taking part is to have enhanced their reputation as either as an architect, engineer, construction manager/main contractor or specialist trade contractor. The latter being the way to ensure *future* business by having repeat orders from the same client or its recommendation of them to others.

All team-member business firms therefore need to have specific *objectives* for the particular construction project to ensure their business aims are met. However, given the nature of a construction project and the interdependence of the firms to complete their work from time to time, these objectives need to have a degree of *commonality* about them. That is to say, the *collective* objectives of every firm for the project must be supportive of meeting each firm's individual business aim. Disputes in construction projects more often than not arise when one firm seeking to meet its own objectives inadvertently puts another participating firm at a disadvantage and causes it to fail to meet its objectives.

DETERMINING COMMON BUSINESS OBJECTIVES – BENEFITS AND PROBLEMS

In can be argued the prime business aim and objectives to be met in any construction project are those of the client. Any project manager would see that as his or her essential function and would ensure that all efforts are directed towards that end. The fact that the progress of the project does not necessarily mean that all the other participants' business objectives are being met, for one reason or another, seems to be of secondary concern as it is not apparently affecting the project. It is only when a participating firm may finally go out of business during the project that this then becomes a concern to the project as a whole.

The construction industry has unfortunately developed a recent historic reputation for one in which any project may well be expected – and even accepted – to have 'casualties' in business terms. For example, the amount of consideration given to the activity of 'resolving disputes' and 'making/resisting claims' and the growth of skills guidance in undertaking these activities reflects an almost inherent conflict to be expected in any project. The majority of contractual systems are designed to cope with potential conflict and the fact that failure by one party in fulfilling a commitment will result in a disadvantage, usually *financial*, to another.

Currently, it can be a very rare construction project with a very enlightened client that sees the project's aim and objectives to be the business success of every participating firm. More often that not, for instance, the client, and especially the client's professional *financial* advisors, are more concerned that the 'contractor' is not seen to be making too much profit than that it makes any at all. It is interesting that 'contractors' have, by tradition, to declare the profit they are making on top of their costs in any contractual tender price – when nobody else does! It is as if the business success of any participating project firm resulting from a project somehow indicates that the client has not had 'value for money', as the cost could have actually been lower if these firms had not made so much profit!

Setting *common business objectives* which result in every firm making a profit and enhancing their reputations through taking part in the project is an ideal which ultimately should benefit the client. For example it can be the case that:

- a participating firm that knows the project will be profitable for it will perform well and not be 'claims conscious' or seek 'disputes' for trivial reasons

- a participating firm that is financially secure during the course of the project will not suddenly go out of business and not be in a position to complete its work at a crucial project stage
- a participating firm whose business is improved financially and in reputation through the project is likely to be there for another project — either for the same client or with other participating firms — as a well-performing firm to work with in the future.

If the benefit can be seen by all participating firms of setting common business objectives for the project then what might be the obstacles to doing so?

Again traditional attitudes and a complete culture have to be overcome, if there is to be openness between all participating firms in terms of the cost of their involvement and the profit they wish to make. Traditional contractual systems almost implicitly imply that the 'contractors' — that is, those firms who manage and actually produce the physical construction — are not to be trusted, which, in once sense, is why there are 'contracts' anyway. It may also be that because we tend *not* to rigorously plan the actual process of the project in great detail before it starts that there are still many unknown factors that only emerge during the course of the project. Contracts are there as a means of dealing with these if some one is disadvantaged, again usually financially, as these unknown factors become known and inevitably cause the work to cost more and take longer than was envisaged at the outset of the project.

Even the use of other forms of construction project procurement that intend to overcome adversarial attitudes — even to the extent of 'partnering' — of themselves will not necessary remove the ingrained culture of distrust needed to evolve a 'whole-project' — especially a 'single-business' — view. Unless the client or lead participant can create such a view from the very inception of the project it is not likely to happen. However, if it can, then the following concepts may help in such a definition.

DETERMINING COMMON BUSINESS OBJECTIVES – A METHOD AND CONSTRAINTS

A modern view of business promotes the necessity, amongst other things, of *business process improvement* (Harrington, 1991) and *business re-engineering* (Hammer and Champy, 1998) through a number of common key themes. These are that, in order to survive the highly competitive market economy of the late twentieth/early twenty-first centuries, *any* business needs to:

- become *customer focused* in everything that it undertakes
- develop a *deep understanding of all its processes* and how they relate to each other in producing its final product or service
- listen to those who work for it and *empower them* as their 'front-line' people are the only ones who can satisfy their customers
- embark on a *non-stop process of continuous improvement* by *continually benchmarking* itself against the best practice of similar businesses
- have *dedicated and passionate leadership* from its senior people
- continually train and educate its staff in best practices derived from all the above.

Winning, satisfying (or even 'delighting') and keeping customers through a customer-focused, employee-empowered and continuously improving process could sum up how businesses will be successful in the near future.

It is therefore interesting to take these principles developed for a *permanent* single 'business' and see how well they would map on to what in effect would be the *temporary multiple* 'business' of the construction project. To begin with, the very fact that projects are 'temporary' in their existence might be a distinct advantage in achieving modern business objectives. One of the major problems in any business improvement or re-engineering process is the extent of organizational and structural *change* needed for current — and often deeply ingrained — practices in any firm. In the construction project no such organizational structure exists; it is created anew each time. Even participating firms that are used to working on projects are themselves often highly flexible in their structure because they have to be to meet the needs of very different 'one-off' projects. The construction industry itself knows instinctively how to manage 'change', as it is doing it all the time through project-based work! If the project is to be viewed as a 'whole business' then it can be 'designed', and not '*re*designed', from new!

With regard to being 'customer focused', again there is a distinct advantage in that the 'customer' is a very obvious 'client' whose needs and expectations can be clearly identified through the project briefing process. It can be further argued that in fact the sole purpose of the project itself is to meet the needs of the client so that in a business sense a construction project is clearly driven by the needs of the 'customer' in the form of the client. However, there are some aspects of modern business improvement concepts that are not readily mapped to the construction project and its traditional cultural setting, in that:

- there is seldom time at the inception of a construction project to develop how the general *processes* of one firm relate to that of another in completing that particular project
- the workers in a project, especially the construction workers, are seldom involved in design decision-making and do not necessarily feel *'empowered'*, as they are usually required to work to a preordained specification and its implicit work process
- because of the 'one-off and ongoing' nature of a project and the fact that work is done that is not necessarily repeated, it can be difficult to have a *process of continuous improvement* by *continually benchmarking* within the life of the project itself
- with the exception of very enlightened clients using appropriate procurement methods who can actually provide *passionate leadership* for the project and all its participating firms taking part, a traditionally procured project is actually 'leaderless'!
- it is usually accepted that all those who work on a construction project — be they designers or constructors — are trained and educated *generally* in their profession or trade and that it is not necessary to train or educate them for a particular project.

Therefore, to set up a construction project as a 'whole business' entity that will be beneficial to all those taking part, the above constraints of traditional project practice need to be removed in that, as far as is practical:

- the interactions between all participating firms' *processes* need to be clearly understood, defined and controlled from project start-up to completion
- the actual workers involved in the construction design and production need to be *empowered* to make decisions about their own work and be responsible for its standard
- through the above 'process control', *continuous improvement* should always be sought and implemented
- clear and decisive *leadership* should always be given by an identified person as the project proceeds
- special training and education for any workers at any time needs to be identified and given *before* they start their specific design and production work.

Once the above is in place, by removing the traditional constraints of practice, a 'whole business system' for the project can be identified and put into place.

DEFINING A 'WHOLE BUSINESS SYSTEM' FOR A CONSTRUCTION PROJECT – THE PARTS AND THEIR RELATIONSHIP

The most effective way to ensure that all firms participating in a construction project share *common* business objectives is to get them to see the project itself as a *whole* business to which they belong. Unless they can do this any one of them is always likely to feel that it as a firm is losing out in business terms to the benefit of the others. Or that others are succeeding at its expense – literally!

In effect, this entails 'designing' the project as a business and uses the same approach as if '*re*designing' an existing business. Only the process can start from a clean slate without the problems involved in trying to redesign a business that already exists (Cornick and Broomfield, 1996). The design of the whole business system starts with the fundamental need of any business, which is to secure its income.

Any business needs to ensure that the payments for its good or services are continuous and current in order to maintain a good cash flow, which reduces the need for borrowing, allows payment to creditors to be prompt (which maintains 'goodwill') and provides a general feeling of comfort for both the business and its supporting bank or other financial institutions. Maintaining good cash flow by prompt payment for services provided can be difficult, as often much 'work' has to be carried out by the business before the service can be seen to have been provided. This can be particularly true where the service is in a 'project-based' business environment – such as construction – in which customers/clients need to see the outcome of a very great deal of 'work' before they have enough confidence to pay anything.

Whether the 'service' provided for a client in the construction project is 'design', 'project management', 'construction management', 'specialist trade contracting' or any other specialism, the particular firm must have the following prime aim as a business:

- to provide its service in such a manner as to ensure that its 'client' pays it promptly because the client is so satisfied that it would wish to engage the firm again and recommend its engagement to others.

All parts of the designed system should be directed at achieving this end. Any system can be described as a collection of interacting processes which has a set of generic 'inputs' that will result in an 'output' — in this instance the one just described. How well the system's process performs will be dependent on the completeness of each generic input and any subinput. The first and vital input to the process of a system that provides any service will be *people*. The applied skills and knowledge — whether they be for 'design' or 'trade operation' — of the firm's people will be the essential means by which a service that satisfies the client will be performed. If people do not have the skills and knowledge to satisfactorily carry out the work the firm requires of them then the firm needs to provide the necessary *training* to make up for the particular lack of skill or knowledge. If they do have the skills and knowledge but do *not* satisfactorily carry out the work for the firm then other parts of the system are lacking. The first, and most critical, generic input to the system is therefore:

- people applying skills and knowledge consistently and conscientiously to their work with training support as necessary.

The ISO 9000 series approach to 'quality' is one in which any firm's management system is demonstrated primarily by described and documented *operational procedures*. That is to say, how various tasks that comprise work are carried out in terms of the types and sequence of activities, the people involved and the various 'outputs' involved. Often resisted as being inhibitory of initiatives, *documented* operational procedures provide a useful description of how people's work is carried out collectively and can be used to train newcomers in the way a firm works. A described operational procedure also forms a basis for formally and systematically reviewing how what is currently being done in work can be improved as a result of internal or external feedback. The requirement of these standards provides both the incentive and the basic approach for any firm to understand its core and supporting processes in carrying out the work it needs to do to provide the service or product required by its client or customer. The second generic input to the system is therefore:

- work processes that are defined as procedures and instructions evident to all the people so that they are understood, can be analysed for 'cause and effect' of work output and be described in such a way that they can be openly designed and changed for improvement.

In all current business improvement initiatives – such as Total Quality Management (TQM) – the notion of 'measure' is paramount. However, exactly *what* is being measured needs careful consideration. The essential information to be derived from any 'measurement' concerning a firm will concern *how much* or *how many?* For example, if the number of customer complaints is reducing then it might be argued that the people's work processes are improving. A similar deduction might be made about a manufacturing process if the number of 'defects' is almost zero. In order to make comparisons with other similar firms about any aspect of work, as with best-practice 'benchmarking', some sort of 'measurement' needs to be made. 'Measurement' after any business's work process has been carried out, that is the say to result of process *outcome*, implies the need for some sort of 'performance standard' to be set and to be aimed at by people carrying out the work. All 'quality control' approaches over the last 25 years have tried to move the focus away from having a 'measure' by which an outcome of a process is either accepted or rejected to one in which 'performance standards' are set for the process itself. A 'performance standard' is equivalent to a constancy of purpose, for example 'zero defects' or 'right first time', for the work itself, as defined by procedures and instructions for a process objective as agreed with an internal or external 'customer'. This means that an individual process, and consequently the system of processes as a whole, can be 'assured' for a known intended outcome.

That is the aim and intent of all 'quality assurance' (QA) systems for product and service businesses. However, a performance standard – which must embrace some idea of 'measure' – must also be realistic to be expected to be achievable. To be this, the standard must recognize the level of skills and knowledge of the people involved and the physical environment in which the work process is carried out. Finally, 'measures' can be used to understand any work process itself to determine whether that process is 'under control' or not. Statistical process control (SPC) was fundamental to the Deming approach to quality (Walton, 1989), and tells any firm about 'variation' in its processes which causes unwanted outcomes. The third generic input to the system is therefore:

- performance standards that provide a constancy of purpose for every work process and are realistic and appropriately 'measurable' for the people involved.

All modern firms, regardless of their type of business, require an ever-increasing amount of *information* to be stored, retrieved and processed in their operations. With firms that are concerned with 'service', it could be argued that all the work processes are solely concerned with information as both their inputs and their outputs. What is produced is information as the actual 'product'. Equally, the mechanisms or 'tools' with which the people carry out their work are those that can deal — by one means or another — with information generation, exchange and storage. Those firms that serve the construction industry deal with information that begins with defining a construction 'need' and which then becomes added to by a variety of specialists through a series of project phases until the construction itself is physically realized. Although the information that each specialist firm basically deals in is different — for example, design standards by architects and engineers and construction operation time duration and sequence by construction managers — it is nonetheless *information* that their people both work with and have to exchange to carry out their work as the project progresses.

Access to a wide range of relevant and current 'general' information — be it 'technical', 'commercial' or 'legal' — is also vital if any of the project specialist firms is to carry out its work efficiently. Timely and accurate 'project-specific' information exchange with the other firms involved is necessary if they are to carry out their work as part of a team effectively. Both their costs and the overall project cost to the client in total will be dramatically affected by each organization's access to and exchange of 'general' and 'project-specific' information. The fourth and final generic input to the system is therefore:

- efficient information access and effective information exchange methods internally and externally with other firms with whom a firm has to carry out its work as part of a team.

In summary, the above four parts of any business system have to be in place for that business to achieve its aim. This applies to each particular business firm taking part in a client's project — whoever the 'client' is, even if it is one of the firms itself. These distinct parts each have an effect on one another if the system is to function holistically. If one part is missing — or even deficient — then the system as a whole will fail so that, for example:

- *people* cannot apply their skills and knowledge if *processes* are not clearly defined

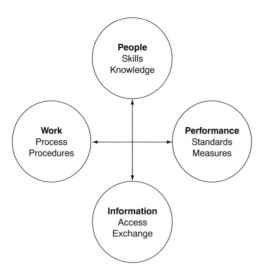

Figure 6.1. Interaction of generic inputs to business system

- *processes* cannot be carried out effectively if *performance standards* are unrealistic
- *performance standards* cannot be set if appropriate *information* is not available
- *information* cannot be accessed or exchanged if *people* do not have the appropriate skills and knowledge to generate it

and so on.

Given that this 'set' of four generic inputs (Fig. 6.1) to the business system applies to every firm that takes part in a construction project – and that a deficiency in each or any causes the 'system' to fail – it can also be taken that the same 'set' can apply on three different, but related levels. These can be considered to be:

- *technical* – which concerns the technology that the particular firm works with in terms of its work output, for example a cladding system
- *financial* – which concerns the particular costs incurred and fees that can be charged for the particular firm's contribution to the project, for example an architectural practice for providing a design service
- *human* – which concerns the particular type of people employed by the firm and their skills, knowledge and motivation, for example a trade operative or professional designer.

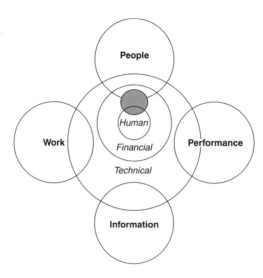

Figure 6.2. Business system input/level relationship, with the human/people 'pivotal point' indicated in grey

When all or any of these three levels are related to the four generic inputs, it can be seen, for example, that *information access or exchange* can be applied to 'technical', 'financial' or 'human' factors. Also, *work process or procedure* can be applied to these factors — for example the methods used for *financial* control — and so can *performance standard or measure* — for example to the required level of accuracy needed for a *technical* detail — and *people skills or knowledge* — for example to the *financial* reward for the firm providing training. What is therefore pivotal between the levels and the inputs is the *human factor* and the *people* input (Fig. 6.2), thus emphasizing the importance of people as human beings in the whole business system and making them the key to success in all of the generic inputs at all of the levels. So, for example, with regard to the 'performance standard' generic input at *any* level, such 'standards' can only ultimately be consistently realized by the care and attitude of the people carrying out the work. Similarly, the 'skills and knowledge' generic input can only be effectively applied by people doing work if they wish to apply it in a positive and continuous manner.

It is also at each of these three levels that the connection can be made between the business system of each participating organization and the construction project itself when viewing it as a business system in its own right. For example, the construction project has an intended *technical* outcome both as a physical assembly and as its end use purpose. So a 'school' will comprise a particular assembly of building technologies to support the 'technology' of education. And so too will the *financial* outcome be a result of how an individual firm's costs and the project costs are managed. Finally, to complete the business system, the four inputs need to be linked to the three levels through practical mechanisms that are familiar in making any firm that is 'in business' work. These four mechanisms are also the practical means by which the firm whose 'business' is construction can be related to the project itself in business terms. They are as follows.

Policy and objectives — which are to inspire the use of the system

These are the *internal* mechanisms which are designed — and continually *re*designed — to meet particular *external* demands from the market, the law, etc.

Organizations and responsibilities — which are to make people accountable

The organization and responsibilities ensure the policies and objectives are implemented and kept under review for *re*design as required and enable the system to be evaluated for continued effectiveness.

Interacting processes — which translate input into output

There are *core* processes that are directly involved in translating the client/customer needs into cash in the bank; there are *support* processes that serve, sustain and improve the core processes; and there are *key core or support* processes.

Records — which become the corporate memory

These are data and information that become accumulated knowledge from operating the system and are an accumulating asset.

The way is which these four mechanisms link both the levels and fundamental inputs, and their direct relationship to the latter is shown in Fig. 6.3. The whole business system can now be seen as an arrangement of familiar parts of an individual firm's own business. The mechanisms, levels and generic inputs can now all be related within any one firm but could also now be related to the business system of any other firm involved in the project.

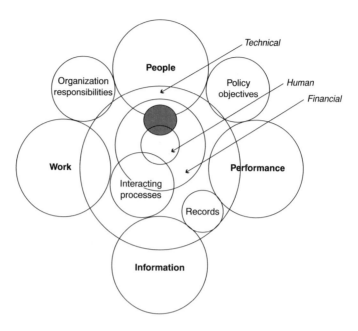

Figure 6.3. The whole business system

DESIGNING A CONSTRUCTION PROJECT AS A WHOLE BUSINESS SYSTEM

In order to get to a position for considering the construction project as a *whole business system*, each part of each participating firm's own system needs to be logically related that of another's. For example, *information* access/exchange and *records*, as shown in Fig. 6.3, have a vital interaction both for the project as a whole and for each participating organization. This is because most of each firm's actual work process input/output comprises the access to and generation and exchange of information. Similarly, *people* are also a vital link between firm and firm as it is through their cooperation, consultation and coordination — by and large on a human level — that decisions are made and problems overcome throughout the course of a construction project. Observations of practice over recent years would seem to suggest that it is the 'human factor' in any project that is crucial to success, and that unless that is fostered in a positive manner all other, 'non-human' systems will be of little use in contributing to success. In fact any aspect of the 'non-human' systems — for example too much paperwork — can actually inhibit good human relations. The importance of interactions is such that, for example, if true 'partnering' between firm and firm is to be realized, 'facilitating' people in the project team to get rid of former 'distrust' and work together in a more positive manner is necessary. Therefore, the generic inputs of each firm's own whole business system, *information* and *people*, are the two that need to directly link and interact in the whole business system for the project. With regard to *work* and *performance standard*, these remain as very much part of each individual firm's own whole business system. This is because 'work' — and the 'performance standard' it requires — is special to each *type* of firm involved in a construction project. For example, the 'work' of an architect or engineer in concept designing is very different from the 'work' of a specialist trade contractor in detail designing and physically assembling an elemental part — even though the 'work' of the latter is required for the actual realization of the 'work' of the former. Therefore, the generic inputs of each firm's own whole business system, *work* and *performance standard*, are the two that have indirect links through *people* and *information* to the whole business system for the project. The way in which the familiar parts may be related to each firm's and the project's whole business system would be as follows:

- the *policy and objectives* and *organization and responsibilities* of each firm would be adapted in part to suit that of the project (for example each firm would have its own 'objectives' for the particular project with which it was involved, which would have to integrate with those of the other participating firms)
- the *interacting processes* would be the way in which the 'output' of one person's work in any firm would become the 'input' to one person's work in another firm
- *records* would become the information as the 'output' of the work of each person in a firm as well as the project and 'record' both the information 'product' — for example, drawings, specifications and meeting minutes — and the information 'process' — for example, how and why decisions were made (the latter being useful to show compliance with health, safety and environmental impact legislation as well as to provide process feedback for future projects).

These familiar parts can therefore be seen to be applicable to both firm and project, and the 'quality plan' mechanism from the ISO 9000 quality standard can be used to map them from an individual firm's corporate management system to the project management system as a whole. The generic inputs, familiar parts and levels can now be described as a whole business system for the project with a firm-to-firm relationship. These firm-to-firm relationships will obviously be from

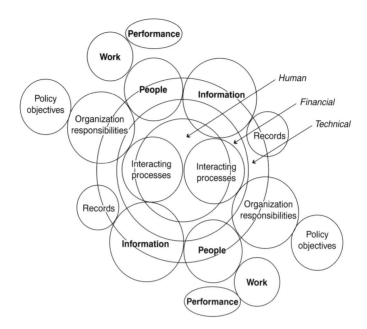

Figure 6.4. The whole business system for the project: firm A, left; firm B, right

each to each, and more or less intense depending on the phase of the project. How a firm-to-firm relationship can be described is shown in Fig. 6.4.

From Fig. 6.4 it can be seen that the way in which the whole business system works for the project is that:

- the people who work in firm A produce information for the people in firm B so that that can carry out their work in producing information for the people in firm A or firm C, and so on

- the people who work in firm A, firm B, firm C, etc., do so to a performance standard that is appropriate to their type of firm's work but which is also dependent on the information they receive from another firm

- the policies and objectives of firm A are likely to differ from those of firm B, and will influence the way in which their people work producing information for each other in order to fulfil the policy and objectives of the project as a whole

- the interacting processes between firm A and firm B, firm B and firm C, etc., should ensure that the people in the other firm can carry out their work to an acceptable performance standard, and

100

the process task sequence between firms is of critical importance in terms of meeting all time, cost and quality requirements
- the whole system works continually and iteratively in its parts and between firms on the human, technical and financial levels.

Ideally, the 'process' combination of different firms on a construction project should be done in such a way that each firm can succeed as a 'business'. That is to say, every participating firm should make a profit and have its reputation enhanced through taking part in the project. Whether that happens or not will by and large depend on the procurement method and project and information management approaches used to carry out the construction project. These aspects, like the important *human* aspect, are dealt with in their own right in various other chapters.

IN CONCLUSION

The 'bottom line' from a business point of view for every firm taking part in the project is to make money and enhance its reputation to ensure future 'customers'. Satisfying not only the client but all the other team-member firms with whom they have to work is important in that all may at some time need to consider, for a future project, the particular type of firm to be selected.

In determining common business objectives there are:

- *benefits* in that each participating firm will know it is financially secure during the project and will financially improved after it; this project will eliminate the need for them to be 'claims conscious' and counter to a positive project culture
- *problems* because the traditional 'culture' of the industry is one in which being appointed on a lowest price on the basis of low margins, and the consequent need for all firms to be 'claims conscious' to achieve profit, or sometimes just to cover costs — but this is gradually changing through 'partnering' approaches
- *methods* borrowed from business practice improvement which encourage all participating firms to be 'customer' focused, have a deep understanding of all their processes, empower their 'front-line' people, have a non-stop process of continuous improvement by continually benchmarking and have passionate leadership from their senior people

- *constraints* still exist in that all the features described in the *methods* above are counter to current traditional practice, for example tradesmen usually are given specifications to follow rather than being able to make a contribution to a solution.

A 'whole business system' for a construction project can be designed that formalizes the interaction between the business systems of each participating firm in terms of its policy, objective, organization, responsibilities, interacting processes and records, all of which operates on human, technical and financial levels. The 'whole-business' process design should ensure that each firm succeeds as a business through participating in the project and could, given goodwill by project team members, work with appropriately supporting procurement methods that encourage cooperation.

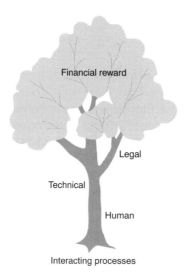

A whole business system. Interacting processes on human, technical and legal levels to support financial reward

7

A team as a temporary organization — getting the right arrangement

INTRODUCTION

In Chapter 2, we suggested that any design or construction organization — regardless of size or type — can only carry out its day-to-day business by becoming involved in a construction project *team*. It will need to seek out client organizations that will have a definite 'business case' for carrying out a particular project. In Chapter 3 we suggested the generic composition of any construction project team and that it comprised not only the commissioning client and main design and construction disciplines, but also all the other stakeholders that would become directly or indirectly involved in the project over time. In Chapters 4 and 5 we suggested that the diversity of people, cultures, disciplines and stakeholders all need to be considered and dealt with in order to create a cohesive, performing construction project team. In Chapter 6, the notion that a construction project could be viewed as a 'whole business system' was proposed and that this was the only way to ensure that all project participants subscribed to common business objectives.

In this chapter we consider how the construction project team is a *temporary* organization and all that is implied by that fact. As with *businesses* in Chapter 6, the mapping is from *permanent* organizations as they can have all the same essential features as a *temporary* organization even though the latter only exists for a comparatively brief period of time.

THE NATURE OF ORGANIZATIONS – THE ESSENTIAL FEATURES

Organizations comprise a collection of people brought together for a purpose and can be groups, companies, corporations, department, plant, etc. (Harrington, 1991) The definition can obviously be applied to a project, the only difference being that the former definitions tend to be permanent – at least for as long as the business itself lasts in a particular form. The essential commonality between all 'organizations' is that:

- there is a *structural arrangement* which determines its parts in terms of processes and people and their relationships (which is both *formally explicit* and *informally implicit* because of the tendency of people to 'skirt around' formal systems)
- there is an *implicit culture* which determines the way work is carried out in terms of approaches, attitudes and beliefs (which is hard to define except as an *ethos* or *spirit* probably created almost sub-conciously by the group 'leaders').

This adds up to a means by which a product or a service is delivered to an 'internal' or 'external' customer.

In a *permanent* organization the above features become engrained and entrenched, basically because human beings, whilst constantly seeking variation, also have a strong desire for security and certainty – especially where the need to earn a regular income is concerned! Changing – or even considering changing – an organization's *structural arrangement* – by altering processes, changing a part of it in size and composition and changing the relationships that exists between the parts inevitably puts somebody's existing position or work under question. New leaders being brought in with new attitudes and approaches can be equally unsettling. However, business process re-engineering (Hammer and Champy, 1998) is about doing just that if it means that the product or service can be delivered cheaper, faster, to a high standard and to more customers than before!

The lesson from this is that it is crucial to get the *right structural arrangement and implicit culture* to suit the purpose of any organization at any time as soon as posssible. The *culture* of the organization will

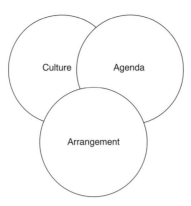

Figure 7.1. A culture, agenda and arrangement essential for a project organization

become established very quickly; having to change it will be difficult and the change itself will be unsettling.

By combining the above features, any 'organization' will also have an *agenda*, which, if it is made absolutely clear to all who work for the organization, is a statement of where together they are going and how they are going to get there (Crosby, 1997). The agenda, which should incorporate such things as the organization's vision and mission, must be set by leaders by design – or another and less desirable one will be set by others by default. Crosby uses the analogy of a cruise to illustrate such an agenda in that the brochure clearly lists the 'vision' of the cruise and all the stopping places, what is going to happen at them, and what is going on in between whilst sailing between them. From this clear 'agenda' all the necessary work to be done, how and where, can be planned with confidence by the people concerned.

Out of all the combined structural-arrangement, implicit-culture and agenda features of organizations (Fig. 7.1), it is the *implicit culture* that is the most significant and either directly, or indirectly, influences the other two. The literature on organization culture is growing and, as referred to in Chapter 5 about clients, it is not necessarily easy to rigorously define. However, different types of organizational cultures can be broadly catagorized as being determined in their character as follows (Handy, 1997):

- the *power* culture, where a strong control is exercised on the organization from a central source, usually an individual
- the *role* culture, where the organization is controlled by a 'bureaucracy' of procedures and rules from a narrow band of senior management

- the *task* culture, where the organization is task-focused and controlled through distributing the power downwards through networks which offer flexible response
- the *power* culture, where the power lies with individuals, or groups of individuals, as person-orientated clusters; this is the way that most professional practices of various disciplines operate.

The factors that influence whether any organization can be considered as either one type of culture or another are such things as history and ownership, size, technology, goals and objectives, the environment and the people. Size can be the most influential factor in that large organizations are more formal, which can be seen by members as offering more potentially friendly and secure places to be. Large organizations can also be thought to be more efficient but more authoritarian by their members. Technology, although important, does not necessarily influence a culture one way or another but rapid changes in technology tend to require a *power* or *task* culture, and a *role* culture supports interdependence and coordination where the technology demands them.

The organization's goals and objectives can both be influenced by the culture and influence it. A *power* or *task* culture supports growth; *role* culture more easily monitor quality and provide places to work and centres of employment. The environment, whether 'economic', 'market', 'the competitive scene' or 'geographical/social', can be crucially important in determining the culture. Different nationalities prefer different cultures depending on the 'individualism' or 'collectivism' of different country cultures — the Anglo-Saxons favouring the former. Market changes and the need for diversity can be best coped with by a *task* culture, while a *role* culture may best suit standardization needs. The *power* culture best reponds to threats of whatever kind that come from the environment.

Finally, and most importantly, it is the impact of an organization's culture on the people who are its members that will influence their job satisfaction, motivation and ultimately individual performance. It has been hypothesized, but not necessarily proven, that:

- people who cannot cope with ambiguity and need security prefer *role* cultures
- people who need to establish their identity can do so best in a *power* or *task* culture in which they can make an impact with their talents and skills
- people with low levels of personal resources are likely to be more comfortable in organizations that have a *role* culture.

Culture, structural arrangement and agenda, all of which may be more or less important, then comprise the nature of any *permanent* organization — either by 'design' if it is restructuring or by 'default' if it has not been considered over a long period of time and just happens.

If this is the inherent nature of the *permanent* organization, then how can the *temporary* organization of the construction project be best designed to ensure the right *arrangement*, make sure the right *culture* is created form inception and maintained to completion, and make sure that the right *agenda* is known and applied by all the participants?

DESIGNING THE RIGHT TEMPORARY ORGANIZATION — MATCHING THE PROJECT OBJECTIVES

It is ironic that at a time when the UK construction industry is being exhorted to look at manufacturing for ideas for improvement, in terms of 'organizational' development it may actually be at the forefront. The manufacturing industries, and in fact all companies that provide services, are inevitably being taken down the road towards far more fluid, flexible and even 'project-based' organizations. The constant pressure to change to meet ever higher customer demands and an increasingly uncertain economic environment is leading major companies to have organizations that loosely connect independent workers. These new types of 'employees' can no longer rely on the promise of a long-term career with any firm as a reward and are therefore becoming highly skilled and knowledgeable individuals whose 'services' the company buys as and when it needs them. These changes lead to the importance of what has been described as 'emotional intelligence' in workers for the new workplace — as old qualities and assessments of personal worth for reward no longer apply (Goldman, 1998). The move towards an increasingly project-based and 'virtual' organization for all companies seems to be an irreversable trend — but that is how construction projects have *always* been!

Because a construction project is novel and 'one-off', its *temporary* organization can be designed 'from a blank sheet of paper'. There is a further advantage in that, in terms of having 'customer-focused' objectives, the organization's 'customer' can be clearly identified in the form of the project's commissioning client. However, the very real danger is that, unless considered from the very inception of the project, its organizational *arrangement, culture and agenda* can just happen by default as the project very rapidly evolves under pressure of time. The firms and their people who join the project — especially the specialist trade contractors — have traditionally been brought into the project on the basis of the lowest tender — rather than because they 'fit' into a pre-designed organizational arrangement, culture and agenda for the project.

If the temporary organization is to be positively designed to support the objectives of the client's project, a summary of *cultural/arrangement* influences can be a useful staring point. These are that certain *cultures* favour certain *arrangements* and vice versa as follows:

- power culture — a 'web' arrangement (all people to all people through an individual 'head')
- role culture — a 'temple' arrangement (all people in lines to a 'head')
- task culture — a 'net' arrangement (some people to some people in lines)
- person culture — a 'net' arrangement (all people as individuals).

It can be seen that each of them can, in some way or another, be generally applicable to any construction project. The other factor that needs to be brought into the equation is that each participating firm, including the client, will already have one of these culture/arrangement combinations implicit in its own organization.

For example, the *task culture* with a *'net' arrangement* might seem to be the most obvious generally, as it best supports projects where the work is very task orientated and people are linked in particular 'lines' for communication in support of those tasks. On the other hand, a construction project with a strong client or project manager who definitely leads, or a strong lead architect or engineer, reflects the *power culture* with a *'web' arrangement*. Another major influence on the project organization design can be that the *task culture* with a *'net' arrangement* best supports innovation where 'changing things' is required — which is what is happening in a construction project as it evolves.

With regard to the types of firms that take part in a project, design, cost, project management and construction management consultancies are best typified by the *person culture* and *'cluster' arrangement* of individuals who almost act as individual consultants on their particular project. However, it would be easy to find large consultancies and contractors with *role cultures* and a *'temple' arrangement* to cope with their 'bureaucracies' or, equally, small consultancies and contractors with *power cultures* and a *'web' arrangement* eminating from a strong, charismatic founder/leader.

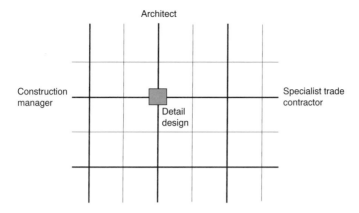

Figure 7.2. A net arrangement linking the architect, construction manager and specialist trade contractor for detail design to suit a production task in a task culture

Therefore it would seem that generally a *task culture* with a '*net*' *arrangement* (Fig. 7.2) would best suit the intended culture for the 'temporary' organization of a construction project.

The challenge for project leadership would be to ensure that any other culture and arrangement in any of the three participating firms in Fig. 7.2 did not inhibit the effective accomplishment of the task of creating the right culture and arrangement for the project. If the arrangement of the people is correct in terms of relationships, with the right overriding culture, then the next step is to ensure it is reinforced by effective and efficient working practices.

DEFINING THE RIGHT WORKING PRACTICES – THE ROLE OF QUALITY ASSURANCE AND WORK BREAKDOWN STRUCTURE

Quality assurance systems based on the ISO 9000 standard help to define the right working practices for the appropriate project arrangement through:

- requiring each organization that takes part and claims to be quality assured to define its individual processes, for which it will have formal procedures describing who does what and where and how, in relationship to someone's work in their *own* organization (for example the designers 'designing')

- requiring those organizations to demonstrate how they apply their processes through procedures to a particular project through a 'quality plan' (for example the construction manager's 'construction work planning').

If the quality plan for each organization is coordinated with those of the other organizations then a 'quality plan' for the whole project is created, which, in effect, is a process work 'map' of how each organization's procedures interrelate to provide a whole-team effort (Fig. 7.3). A more detailed analysis of each of the processes shown in Fig. 7.3 by each organization would show the required 'inputs' from another team-member organization so that its work process could produce the 'output' as an 'input' to another team-member organization's process – and so on (Cornick, 1991). Each process will comprise 'tasks' and 'subtasks' that can be described in terms of the required skills/knowledge, performance standard, procedures, information technology and information 'inputs'.

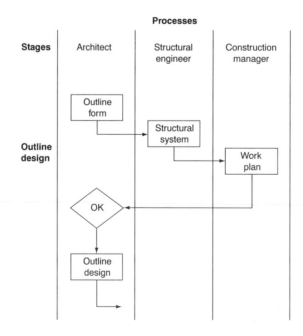

Figure 7.3. A process map linking the architect, structural engineer and construction manager for a team process working through a 'quality plan'

Using such a standard process model is a way of ensuring that all 'task inputs' are clearly identified so they have no deficiencies (for example insufficient available 'skills') in any of them that would result in a 'defective' information output to the next team-member organization's 'task' and 'subtasks'.

The application of other project management tools such as the work breakdown structure (WBS) (Spinner, 1997) would further clarify the picture of a totally integrated *teamworking* process for the project organization arrangement. A WBS comprises 'tasks' that need to be done, the order in which they should be done, 'subtasks' that comprise a 'task' and the 'milestones' to be reached at the end of each. Using a simple numbering system, a WBS of the teamworking described above could look like the following:

1000   Agree outline design
       1100   Agree outline form
       1110   Produce outline form for building requirements (by the architect)
       1120   Structural system for structural requirements (by the structural engineer)
       1130   Work plan for cost/time requirements (by the construction manager)
       1199   Milestone. Agreed outline form
1200   Agree spatial layout
Etc.

The 'milestones' are put into either a Gantt chart, which describes the 'tasks' in terms of duration and place in time, or a Pert chart, which describes the tasks in terms of their dependency relationship, to meet the desired timescale of the project. If the 'tasks' are also linked back to the individual team-member organizations' processes, then a complete resource–task–time picture emerges that describes

- how each person's work is related to that of another team member
- the degree of dependence of each team member on the other team members
- how their work *together* as a team achieves the *objectives* of the project,

the project *objectives* being the project's temporary organization's agreed collective *agenda*.

DEFINING THE RIGHT 'AGENDA' FOR A TEMPORARY ORGANIZATION – THE PROJECT'S AIM, OBJECTIVES AND ETHOS

In terms of both *culture* and *arrangement*, it can be seen that a construction project tends, by its very nature, to be 'task' orientated. That is to say that each person involved, right down to an individual staff member in a particular firm, can see a 'task' to be done. Also, the 'task' they have to accomplish is one which they are very used to doing in general terms and they have the skill and knowledge to do it with very little supervisory guidance. This applies equally to a designer and a tradesman who are used to carrying out a particular skill-based task – for example designing building elevations and assembling joinery items, respectively.

The real challenge comes, and usually problems arise, when these individuals fail to realize how what they do well *generally* needs to be *specifically applied* to a *particular* project. The failure in perception and resulting 'defective' work comes not as result of design or trade skill incompetence but as a result of *mis*understanding the specific operating and aesthetic requirements of the project. A simple example might be that although a designer and a carpenter are both capable of specifying and making joinery for most operational use, but they may fail to appreciate the robustness needed for a specific use.

It is therefore important that all who take part in the project understand the *specific* needs of the project in order to inform their work – before they begin. Understanding the specific needs of the project through an organizational *agenda* will mean that any such an agenda should comprise at the very least

- the project vision and mission (which can be 'to ...'),

from which should come

- the key milestones in the project's life cycle (which can be 'to ... by ...')
- the critical role of each participating firm (which can be 'to ... as ...')
- the critical constraints of other stakeholders (which can be 'to ... because ...')

and, in general terms, the desired cooperative spirit and ethos to be practised between all the team members for it to be considered a success by all participants. Given that both culture and arrangement favour a task-orientated approach, the *agenda* too is supported by this approach. 'Tasks' are what are most easily defined in the agenda in that the overall 'mission' could be best described as a task. The essential role that each participant will play will again be best defined in terms of overall tasks. Milestones are also best defined by the accomplishment of particular tasks or sets of tasks.

It would therefore seem that the most natural state of a construction project regarding *culture*, *arrangement* and *agenda* is the focus on tasks and their accomplishment. The necessity in a construction project for the carrying out of a task by one person to be dependent on a task being carried out by another is one of the greatest encouragements to 'team-working' as the natural order of things in the construction industry.

IN CONCLUSION

The purpose of the temporary 'organization' is to obtain *cooperation* from all the individual people in the participating firms if teamworking is to be realized. Cooperation can only come through 'organization' if it is recognized that in any organization there will be a *culture*, an *arrange-ment* and an *agenda* which need to be positively designed and explicit – otherwise they will, by default, be implicit, hidden and at worst counter to client's actual aim and objective for the project.

A culture, arrangement and agenda will all be mutually supportive in that:

- a particular arrangement may create a certain culture and spawn by default a 'hidden' agenda
- a particular culture will demand a certain arrangement and also spawn by default a 'hidden' agenda
- a particular agenda will necessitate a certain arrangement and both will create by default a certain culture.

It follows that all of these three aspects of the temporary organization must be considered together at the very outset of the project – as they all will develop very rapidly in an uncontrolled manner because of the comparatively fast pace at which a project progresses, circumstances arise and situations change.

The 'task-orientated' approach that is a feature of any construction projects lends itself to the natural formation of a particular culture and arrangement. At least this is the ideal.

Finally, the temporary organization will achieve the necessary co-operation by bringing together the right culture, arrangement and agenda for the construction project team.

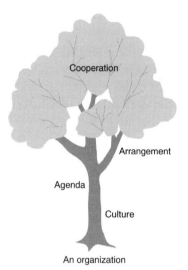

An organizational approach. Arrangement, agenda and culture combine to support cooperation

8

A team as an information exchange — communicating the right messages

INTRODUCTION

In Chapter 2, we suggested that any design or construction organization — regardless of size or type — can only carry out its day-to-day business by becoming involved, either sooner or later, in a construction project *team*. It will need to seek out client organizations that will have a definite 'business case' for carrying out a particular project. In Chapter 3 we suggested the generic composition of any construction project *team* — regardless of project size and complexity — that comprised not only the commissioning client and main design and construction disciplines, but also all the other stakeholders that would become directly or indirectly involved in the project. In Chapters 4 and 5 we suggested that the diversity of people, cultures, disciplines and stakeholders all need to be considered and dealt with in order to create a cohesive, preforming construction project team. In Chapter 6, the notion that a construction project could be viewed as a 'whole business system' was proposed and that this was the only way to ensure that all project participants subscribed to common business objectives. In Chapter 7, the view of the team as a temporary organization was taken so that the culture, arrangement and agenda created were appropriate to the project.

In this chapter we consider how the construction project team needs to act as an effective and efficient *information exchange*, as passing information between the people involved comprises, for the most part,

115

passing 'information' to each other, adding value to it before passing it on. It can be argued that the actual work of the project team is to pass information to each other, adding value at each pass by inputting their own knowledge until it finally reaches its role in project realization. Just as the soccer team passes a ball in order to finally score a goal, so too does the construction project team with information. It also a well-recognized fact that a lot of project *cost* incurred by participants is directly related to the generation and passing of information. Certainly it can be regarded as the *only cost* incurred and charged by the designer, cost advisor and project manager members of the team.

The great interest in information technology applications to the construction project over the past 25 years is derived from the fact if computers can improve the generation and communication of information so too will the project process be improved — especially in reducing wasted cost through ineffective and inefficient information generation and processing. This recognizes and reinforces the fact that it is *information* which is perceived to be the most important aspect of everyone's work in carrying out a construction project.

INFORMATION — WHAT IT IS AND HOW IT IS COMMUNICATED

From the late 1960s when certain 'pioneers', from both the world of practice and that of research, started to consider the impact of computers, methods of information management and exchange in construction projects have been studied in depth. In parallel with these studies have been developments in trying to improve manual-based systems in order to rationalize and coordinate the drawings, specifications, bills of quantities, schedules, etc., used in a construction project. Coordinating construction project information (CCPI, 1986) was seen to be a major step towards a more efficient and economic project process in that experience from practice suggested that

- *un*coordinated information between say the architect's and structural engineer's drawings caused confusion and delays
- *un*coordinated information between say the designer's drawings and specification and the quantity surveyor's bill of quantities caused confusion and extra cost because of unmeasured items
- *un*clear information where too much information was crammed onto production drawings caused costly mistakes by the contractor

and so on.

116

The key to improvement in construction project information was seen to be in its rationalization so that:

- different expressions of elemental data were linked by code — for example the architectural image of a particular element junction would be linked to its textual specification and its measurement in a bill
- different types of information were differently represented, in terms of scale and level of detail, according to whom it was directed — for example a *location* drawing would provide a construction planner or foreman with the overall information for, say an external wall configuration; an *assembly* detail would tell a quantity surveyor for measurement and a specialist trade contractor for site assembly how a window would fit into the wall; and a *component* drawing and *schedule* would tell a specialist manufacturer how the window should be made and, especially, its critical dimensions to ensure it fitted in assembly.

In this way the right person had the right information and only that which he or she needed. Rationalized and coordinated *paper-based* information methods helped in communicating a design solution to component manufacturers, specialist trade contractors and construction managers in 'production' drawings. As these drawings and specifications were also 'contractual' documents for the appointed contractor, the clearer they were the better, to avoid confusion which could lead to disputes and costly delays and claims — and finally law suits, which can be expensive for all concerned!

However, there are many other communication breakdowns in the construction project for which improving 'production' information once design has been decided is not the answer. Many current and past applied and fundamental construction design and management research projects have focused on the need to improve the briefing/designing information interaction (IAI, 1997–1999). For example, communicating the client's business objectives in a project to the rest of the project team at the earliest possible time is considered vital if clients are to be satisfied with the outcome of their projects. If designers can understand the client's business objectives then the client's priorities can be appreciated in decision-making when arriving at solutions.

Equally, the designer needs to be able to communicate to the client how the evolving design is actually meeting all the client's objectives and where it is not, and what are the necessary points of compromise, etc. Unless this information can be adequately communicated in an understandable format (which may not necessarily be 'drawings') then the designer will become committed to design solutions that later may be seen as not meeting all the client's objectives. Design change at a later stage may be resisted, and an unsatisfactory compromise sought and reluctantly accepted by the client, which could increase overall dissatisfaction and lead to a reluctance to pay.

Another major communication 'gap' in construction projects is the undertanding of safe and economic construction implications of proposed designs in the designing/specification phases of the project. This means that 'production' information of, say, a specialist trade contractor's types of assembly needs to be accessible to designers. Unless this information is readily available and reasonably accurate and up-to-date there is a risk that the designer will make decisions, even at outline or scheme, that later have to be changed to make construction practical. Again, this in turn can lead to wasted design effort disputes and claims-seeking — none of which is conducive to project 'team-working' — especially as this information mostly determines the final cost to the client of the designer's design.

Knowing that all the ever-increasing construction laws and good practice guidance have been complied with as design and construction management decisions are being made in the briefing/designing/specification phases of a project is also vital if decisions are to be made that do not have to be changed later. All of this exists is generally available 'data' but needs to be interpreted in relation to the specific needs of the client's programme in the light of the particular client's project as relevant information.

The 'information' most needed to support effective 'communication' between project team members needs to be:

- readily available
- accurate
- complete
- timely
- in a clear format understood by the recipient.

It is not necessarily that which is represented and presented in traditional contractual drawings, specifications and bills.

The most important aspect of any information that is exchanged between project team members is that it supports shared and timely decision-making. If it does not then its lack makes decisions invalid and needing to be changed later. All of this creates wasted time because of rework — in either the design or construction process — and breeds resentment, cause disputes, creates claims and generally makes for dissatisfaction by every team member involved.

SHARING KNOWLEDGE — ADDING VALUE TO INFORMATION

In a previous book one of the authors (Cornick, 1996) proposed that if the full benefits of emerging information technologies are to be realized in construction they should ultimately support the sharing of knowledge between project team members. Knowledge-sharing will only come about if each team member feels that in doing so they will directly benefit. Observation of project practice through much applied research indicates that with the 'adversarial', traditional method of procurement there is a tendency for team members to use their knowledge to defend their position as this is what they are so often forced to do. Unless the right atmosphere of *trust* exists between all project participants through the method of procurement and how it is being project managed, then there is a risk 'knowledge' will be withheld — by whoever for whatever reason.

Given that the right atmosphere of trust exists between the project team members, the actual nature of the information exchange must be right if it is to support the sharing of knowledge. All project team members — be they client, designer, construction manager or a particular specialist — have their own unique knowledge regarding construction related to the project. This knowledge can only be effectively and efficiently applied by the project team members if:

- information they are presented with is in the form they most readily understand and to which they can best apply their specific knowledge
- information they are presented with is complete in terms of all necessary data needed so that their specific knowledge can be applied
- information they are presented with is at the right time with regard to the design and construction management development programme so that the application of their specific knowledge will not mean altering a decision already made, and work done, by another team member.

Unless all the above three criteria are met there is a risk that knowledge is applied incorrectly because:

119

- an incorrect interpretation is made by the recipient
- the information is incomplete
- the information is untimely.

However, if these criteria are all met then the correct knowledge applied at the right time adds value to the information so it can be passed back or passed on to another project team member for the application of *their* knowledge.

For a construction project team to be an effective 'information exchange' the information the members pass to each other must have the application of the other's knowledge *right first time*. Knowledge wasted by team members can have indirect and direct economic consequences in that:

- as their *knowledge* is in effect what they 'trade in', in business terms its 'waste' must be financially *unrewarding* in that what have invested in is not being used properly
- as the application of their knowledge is what they have in effect priced for then having to apply it more than once constitutes work that is *unpriced* for and will increase their costs and reduce their hoped-for profit.

Conversely, unless *appropriate specific knowledge* is applied *right first time* to create information at every exchange then it is also wasted and needs to be passed, again repeating work that is not necessary — and not priced for either.

All team members must be able to contribute their knowledge and feel that it is valued. It can only be valued if it is not wasted. It can only add value to the evolving project process if the means of information exchange allows it to do so in terms of timeliness, completeness and method of presentation.

EMERGING TECHNOLOGIES — WHY THEY WILL SUPPORT PROFITABLE TEAMWORKING

Ever since the 1960s the 'promise' has been that computer applications would improve the design and construction management process in construction — especially in terms of economy and efficiency. Even in the late 1990s that 'promise' has yet to be fully realized and any real and measurable improvements have come about over the last 30 years through changing procurement methods and their supporting management styles — and *not just* through the application of computers.

At the heart of the 'belief about improvement has been the perception that most economic and efficiency problems are caused by a *sequential* — rather than a *simultaneous* — design and production process. That is to say that design is complete before the production implications of the design have been fully understood in terms of cost, quality and time. The result of this has been that inefficient production is built into the design and over-budget tenders require the design to be changed later to achieve economic and efficient production in the subsequent construction process. Or even worse, the contractor uses his or her construction 'knowledge' once site production has begun to create all sorts of claims to overcome the in-built design inefficiencies.

Moving from a *sequential* to a *simultaneous* overall integrated process requires

- a method of procurement that supports this way of working (as discussed in other chapters)
- a method of information retrieval, representation and exchange that allows 'production' implications in terms of cost and time to be fully understood during the design process,

and it is in meeting the latter criterion where the computer as an information technology offers potential support. In applied research projects and actual information technology software development over the past 30 years it has been that capability that has been of interest, explored through research and exploited in actual software package development and production.

However, it has only been in about the last 10 years of computer software development that this 'simultaneous' method of working has become possible using computers in the design and production of construction. In brief, this capability has become available through programming techniques and software languages that enable the computer to represent 'physical objects' in computer-aided design (CAD) systems rather than just as 'lines on paper'. This in turn means that the drawn representation of construction can have 'meaning' in terms of construction process cost and time, so that when assemblies are drawn for design their cost and time implications can be simultaneously calculated and understood. Modern visualization and simulation computer techniques can now also be used to appreciate site assembly processes in terms of work sequence.

Information technology through computers is fast becoming available that will support *simultaneous* design and construction management processes. An international organization, comprising major construction design and construction practices and leading software vendors (IAI, 1997–1999), is defining models of various construction processes which, when translated into future software products linked to CAD, will make such an approach a practical reality. The outcome of this initiative is to have interoperability not only between different software systems but also between the various design and construction project team members as they carry out their design and construction management work processes. This will mean that

- the architect's design data — expressed in terms of configurations of space and material systems form — will be capable of being directly related to
- the engineer's design data — expressed in terms of structural and environmental performances — which will in turn be capable of being directly related to
- the cost controller's or construction manager's resource data — expressed in terms of cost, time and quality — and which in turn can be capable of being directly related back to

the client's cost, time and quality project targets.

The potential for these systems in support of effective and efficient information exchange between project team members is therefore significant. It means that as the knowledge of one member is applied in their work in order to generate a piece of information, that information can automatically have the knowledge of another team member simultaneously applied. For example the architect's form can be immediately related to a cost plan, which can be related to an engineer's structural or services system — and the interactive implications immediately understood. What all this will mean for productive teamworking is that:

- one piece of information becomes *shared* — rather than repeated time and again from different viewpoints using manual paper-based methods
- additional information — for example *structural* design to *architectural* design and *cost* to both — becomes automatically added, adding *value* to the originally generated piece of information
- if, for example, *architectural* design information needs to be modified in the light of the *structural* design and *cost* information, then this can occur immediately with assured applied knowledge.

Therefore the frustration, and often cost, of delay in applying the knowledge before *architectural* design has progressed too far is eliminated. The emerging technologies which will be making their impact early in the next decade will therefore have a profound effect on teamworking — to the economic benefit of both the client and other project design and construction team members.

'VIRTUAL TEAMS' — THE OPPORTUNITIES AND ISSUES

It is a fact of professional practice that, as a team member, each participant's work is very *individual* from his or her own discipline's point of view. There is a *project* architect and engineer from an individual professional practice as well as a *project* manager, cost controller and construction manager, also each from their own practices or companies. Even if these people head up a 'team' back in their own firms, as a *project* team they are very much individuals with their own individual contribution to make. This contribution is based not only on their *specific* knowledge of their own discipline but also the *particular* knowledge of their own personal experience of past projects. Unlike project 'teams' that are created in an individual organization to put in place, say, a new computer installation and who all still belong to the same firm, *construction* project teams comprise individuals who, in effect, represent their own participating firm commercially, but themselves as individuals *professionally*.

It might therefore be argued that the construction project team is in effect a 'virtual' team in that it together has no specific, fixed organizational base nor, as a whole group, any particular loyalty except to the project client. Long before the notion of the 'virtual' team — or even the 'virtual' organization — was considered because of the emerging Internet-based information technologies, *construction* project teams have in effect always been 'virtual' in their normal method of working. In other words a 'team' of individuals is formed so that together they can achieve the aims of a particular client's project. They are also likely, as individuals, to be members of other construction project teams for other clients.

The 'virtuality' of a construction project team lies in the fact that its members actually carry out their work in remote locations and only physically come together for progress meetings as the project evolves through its various phases. Also, they can do their own work — whether that work is 'design', 'construction planning', 'cost controlling' or actual 'production' — unaided by another project team member as long as they already have — or have direct ready access to — *information* that other team members need to provide.

The notion of the 'virtual' organization through future Internet/ intranet computer-based systems that allow real-time networking is therefore something that the construction industry can quite easily embrace (Vincent, 1998). As the 'organization' of the firms that employ the individual team members of different disciplines moves towards that arrangement so the temporary 'organization' of the project itself can naturally follow. Working as a team of different disciplines from remotely located firms — each of which holds a particular discipline's 'knowledge base' — but together in real-time using Internet-based shared applications offers enormous potential for profitable working in that:

- the *project architect* will be able to call on the 'architectural design' knowledge of his or her own firm's experiential knowledge as well as the 'cost', 'construction planning' and 'specialist design' knowledge for making right-first-time decisions
- the *design information* is only generated once on CAD with all the other necessary cost, construction resource and specialist knowledge data automatically linked to it through data and knowledge-base 'object' technology
- the *design change proposals*, which more often than not happen as the project evolves through other circumstances, can be immediately verified in terms of cost, quality and time and recorded as being agreed.

Being able to do all the above will virtually eliminate the cause of all the costly claims for variation that so often have the effect of financial loss to either one or all of the participating project team members.

It will also give the client that certainty of cost, time and quality at the various project phases that is so vital to its own firm's business case for the project itself.

In Conclusion

The ideal information exchange method allows the project team members to share their knowledge openly and at the most opportune time for the client's project. Timely, complete and appropriately presented information is necessary for effective and efficient teamworking. Wasted knowledge and unnecessarily repetitive genera-tion of any piece of information causes frustration and increased costs to team-member firms, with their subsequent loss of profit. This leads to further wasted effort by team members on claims and their resis-tance, with a resulting deterioration of team spirit, in the construction phase of a project.

Emerging information technologies in CAD-related and Internet-based software systems will be supportive of an effective and efficient information exchange method in that:

- individual-discipline team members will be able to work together as and when they need to from the remote locations of their firms during the design, cost control and construction resource planning project phases virtually simultaneously, using shared information
- an *information culture* will be created within the project team, confirming each member's contribution as being the timely pro-duction and transmission of appropriate information rather than the production of 'drawings, specifications, bills and programmes'.

Finally, unless an organization and contractual *culture* can be created that both encourages and rewards knowledge-sharing between all team members, *information technologies* will not be able to produce the above 'promised' realization of themselves. If, however, both are in place then the rewards for every team-member firm will be very significant.

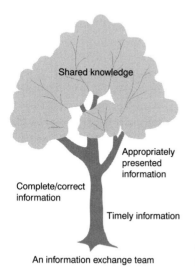

An information exchange team

An ideal information exchange. Timely, correct/complete and appropriately presented information to support shared knowledge

Part 2

CASE STUDIES

Five scenarios are provided in Chapters 9 to 13 which, between them, describe a span of situations to which the issues discussed in Part 1 of the book can be related. The devil is in the detail, as they say, and this is nowhere more true than in construction projects, where success may hinge on a proper and timely appreciation of the human agendas which underlie business cases, as well as policies and plans. Construction project teams — even teams in the figurative sense used in this book — are organic, and behave in a right-brain, intuitive way as well as in accordance with the logical dictates of the left brain.

These case studies draw out some of the team issues which occur in the conception and execution of projects. Each one has a summary of the key issues, and the reader is invited to put him- or herself in the position of a team leader, and consider how to handle these.

The relationship of the case studies to the various chapters in the previous part of the book is indicated in the table below.

	The railway at Berzozil (Chapter 9)	Alminster Town Hall (Chapter 10)	The Ark (Chapter 11)	Argent House (Chapter 12)	Kelso Day Centre (Chapter 13)
Chapter 4: a team of diverse people and cultures	×		×		×
Chapter 5: a team of diverse disciplines and stakeholders	×	×		×	×
Chapter 6: a team of diverse businesses	×	×	×	×	×
Chapter 7: a team as a temporary organization				×	×
Chapter 8: a team as an information exchange	×	×		×	×

9

Case study: the railway at Berzozil

This is an imaginary case study, set in an eastern European state invented for the purpose. The issues raised in it are in some ways typical of the region, but no resemblance to any existing country or district is intended, nor are the events, people or organizations involved intended to represent real ones.

The case study refers to work stages based on the RIBA Plan of Work (RIBA, 1968 onwards).

EuroKonsult SP, an international project management consultancy, won an appointment from the World Bank to develop the potential of the railway network in the eastern European republic of Moesia. The brief of the company was to study all aspects of the railway's operations and its capital holdings. The subproject group on which we will focus – Group B – had the task of reporting on the local centre of Berzozil, which was to be made the subject of a pilot scheme.

BACKGROUND

Moesia is struggling in the postcommunist phase to find its foothold on the economic ladder of the free market. The collapse of the Comecon trade system in 1989, and the consequent exposure of industry to the realities of international competition at real, rather than subsidized, prices, has led to a widespread collapse of old manufacturing industry, and a flood of imports. The currency is subject to constant pressure on the international markets, and there is severe price inflation as government subsidies on fuel and other basic goods are progressively removed. The real value of wages has fallen by 40% in the last year, and many people are poorer than ever before. Nevertheless, there are signs that the tide is turning; the country is stable politically, and there has been considerable foreign investment in modernizing industry; there is a well-educated workforce, even if its older members lack motivation; and the value of the currency is beginning to stabilize.

TRAVEL AND THE RAILWAYS

Travel by train is the traditional and usual means of transport for both individuals and goods over long distances in Moesia. There is a widespread railway network, and the trains are all crowded, so you might conclude that the railway enterprise is in a fortunate position. However, a railway official confides in you that people use the train because for most of them there is no alternative; as they represent a captive market, the railway company, CFM, takes little account of their particular needs, comfort or convenience. 'They might as well be cattle so far as we are concerned', he says with an apologetic shrug. Certainly, both the trains and the stations are in poor repair and habitually dirty. There are long queues at the ticket offices, and connections between trains often involve long delays.

Road traffic in Moesia has increased sixfold since 1990, despite the rigours of the economic situation. Everywhere there are cars, and as many of these are now relatively powerful foreign models, the speed of traffic has increased considerably. Apart from cars, there are also many TIR (long-distance international) trucks. Because of their weight (up to three time the size of the trucks in use before 1989), these vehicles are causing a rapid deterioration of the already poor quality of the road surfaces.

The roads in Berzozil and its district are now too crowded; the main highway from the capital of Moesia to that of a neighbouring republic passes straight through it; this highway is dangerously in need of maintenance; and the hazards of dense traffic and high speeds are added to by the presence of wandering animals, horses and carts (unlit at night), and farm machinery. In short, travel on this road is an experience which few would relish. Nevertheless, those who have access to a car nearly always use it in preference to other forms of transport, and car ownership seems set to continue to increase rapidly.

Berzozil — the main highway to Kiev

Bus travel is not much used for long distances, although there are a lot of local buses. There are also increasing numbers of international coaches, for holidaymakers and guest workers abroad.

BERZOZIL

Berzozil is an industrial centre, which owes its existence to its situation at an important railway junction. Fifty years ago, it was a pleasant market town, with streets of villas and tenement buildings in the elaborate, seventeenth-century style of the area. Industrial development increased the size of the town by a factor of five, and replaced the old buildings with blocks of flats which are, stylistically, no more than the generic socialist design. The approach to the town is dominated at one end of its main street by the derivative modernist Moesia Hotel (1973), and at the other by a large, half-complete Catholic Church, in a postmodern Gothic style.

The industry which gave Berzozil its economic importance is now in decline. Several major operations, including the petrochemical works of SN Berzozolio, have closed altogether. New enterprises, particularly international joint ventures for intensive animal rearing and paper manufacture, are prospering, but some other local industries of inherent quality, such as aircraft repair facilities, are simply ticking over, waiting for better times, or a foreign saviour, to arrive.

Berzozil — main street

Berzozil — station platform

Berzozil — sidings and industrial land

Berzozil — station interior

The town is planned along a long (3 km) main street, with residential areas extending about 1 km either side of it. Industrial sites are situated around the fringe.

The hub of the town is its market, and a few public buildings. There is no defined commercial area, and new enterprises of modest size, such as professional firms, often occupy space in residential blocks, as being the only way of acquiring a space near the centre.

The railway station, and substantial sidings and shunting yards, straddle the western fringe of the town. The main station is about 0·75 km from the main street, linked to it by a broad residential street, the Avenue 3 August. There are a few shops outside the station, but for the most part its surroundings are underused railway property, low-density housing or vacant waste land.

The station comprises a large booking hall, railway offices, a baggage room, a passenger waiting room, a buffet which functions only occasionally and lavatories. There are six lines. There is a pedestrian access tunnel beneath the track to the platforms, but as this is dark and smelly, most people cross the track instead. Outside, there is a taxi rank, and some limited parking, for which a charge is made.

GROUP B AND ITS TASK

The initiators of the venture, and the World Bank as its financial backers, wished to see a thorough demonstration of what could be achieved. Group B had been briefed to:

(1) analyse the present situation
(2) identify ways in which a customer-centred approach to operating the station could be initiated, and begin to demonstrate advantages
(3) advise on the possible strategies for redeveloping the railway station, and develop a timescale taking into account and coping with any disruptive effects of the construction work on the operation of the railway facility
(4) report in principle on the feasibility of developing a new commercial centre for the town on the land adjoining the railway station, including its financing prospects.

GROUP B COMPOSITION

Group B had a core of financial/institutional management skills, and a transportation specialist who had previously been in the team for the

Channel Tunnel railway link project. There was also a commercial surveyor with experience of the regeneration of the London Docklands.

At an early stage, it decided to keep its existing composition, with two additions:

(1) translator
(2) country specialist, with a general understanding of Moesian systems and practices.

These posts were filled by:

(1) an extremely competent Moesian bilingual interpreter, who also became the project's local administrator, called Muine Dischis
(2) a former Foreign Office commercial attaché, with post-1989 experience in a neighbouring eastern European republic.

Specific additional skills were to be supplied by consultants. These were initially identified as:

- transport planner
- town planner
- architect
- civil engineer
- services engineer
- building economist
- telecommunications specialist
- marketing specialist.

During the initial, feasibility phase, all of these would report to Group B, which would have the role of a board of directors. A general project brief was written, and the various consultants were given their own specific, individual instructions.

Consideration was given to the issue of whether to appoint local nationals to consultancy posts, or Westerners. It was felt that local specialists would not have experience, or possibly even adequate knowledge, of the kind of Western models which were likely to be followed, and that therefore it would be better to have a Western team, which would hand over to locals at the implementation stage. All the appointments were made outside Moesia, therefore, except for the building economist, who was a Moesian who had hired in Paris for many years.

The group made frequent trips to Moesia, but generally held its progress meetings in EuroKonsult SP's offices in London or

Maastricht, for convenience. The various consultants, who were mostly London-based, held ongoing dialogues with designated group members, and reported at formal meetings.

The group established relations with local authorities and the railway managers at an early stage. The Mayor of Berzozil, Constantin Plec, and the county manager of the railway system, Antonin Galben, together with the Minister for Inward Investment, Adrian Salmalec, were invited to join a study tour of railway station and land developments in the UK, the Netherlands and France.

GROUP B'S ACTIONS

Analytical report and initial works

The analytical report was published slightly ahead of schedule, in month 4. It identified very encouraging potential for growth in the station itself, recommended the creation of a transport interchange based on the station and produced some basic investment return figures for development of the surplus railway land.

The analytical report was gravely critical of the attitudes of the Railway towards its customers, and recommended immediate and far-reaching changes. These included training all staff in dealing with customers, a promotional campaign to promote goods services, and an immediate phase of work to brighten up the station facilities and improve the long waiting times affecting ticket purchases. In the longer term, it reported favourably on the possibilities of developing the station environs as an office centre to provide for emerging, energetic small businesses which could not find suitable space with a correct image in the old town centre, and a technology park for new light industries.

On the basis of the analytical report, Group B received the go-ahead to begin initial works on improvement of the station including staff training, and to develop the ideas for the creation of a new commercial centre and a technology park.

A contract was placed, after tendering, with Top Trainers, a commercial training organization operating from Manchester, which had recently completed an EU-funded international project involving cultural exchanges within the EU area. Top Trainers' brief was to develop and implement a training project for the 490 staff employed in the Berzozil region, with an emphasis on improving customer relations.

At the same time, the construction consultants were told to proceed to the scheme design stage on the railway station and land. The architect was also instructed to produce some working details and a specification for limited works to improve the appearance of the station in the immediate future.

Within a month, both Top Trainers and the architect had completed their preparatory work so far as they could, and were ready to begin locally.

Training courses were arranged for managers, and short sessions fitted around the working day for other staff, as the national conditions of employment did not allow for training within work schedules.

The architect interviewed a number of local contractors, and placed a contract with the preferred one, after the contractor had revised the specification information into a form with which he was familiar, had it priced by a local economist, and prepared contract documents in the local style. This caused some disquiet at first, as a standard form of international building contract on JCT lines had been intended by the architect. Negotiations revealed such a contract to be incompatible with local law, and incomprehensible to the local parties. The arrangements were reviewed and approved by Group B's own, Paris-based consultant building economist.

Railway station and commercial centre redevelopment

Simultaneously, initial proposals were being prepared by the consultant teams reporting to EuroKonsult in London, for the two major urban renewal programmes. Both Group B and their superior board were keen that the schemes should be at the leading edge of design thinking, and really 'put Berzozil on the map'. Unimaginative, humdrum solutions were quickly ruled out, and a radical relocation of the economic centre of the town to the railway station area was indicated. Good links were secured by way of an enhanced ring road, a public transport interchange based on the station, and a light rail system to new light industrial sites on the old, extensive railway sidings sites.

At this time, publicity was given to the programme at local and national level, with solidarity and goodwill demonstrated by Moesian politicians in newspaper and television interviews. An interview with two of Group B's senior staff appeared in the *International Journal of Project Management*, in which the strategy for the whole programme was sketched out, and a model of the development illustrated.

It was recognized that some financial pump-priming for an ambitious scheme would be required; indeed, this was an integral part of the concept. World Bank finance would cover the creation of the transport interchange, a commercial development of 50 000 m^2 next to the station and enabling works for the redevelopment of the sidings land. The value of this would be reflected in a joint stock foundation company, Berzozil 2000 SRL, in which the shareholding would be 49% to the bank, and 51% to the Moesian state as owner of the land and existing structures. This was a revolutionary development, as previously the state had not allowed any foreign ownership of state land, and indeed had never placed any formal valuation on state-owned real estate.

Progress

It became apparent fairly soon that there were significant differences in expectations, both of standard of workmanship and of performance, between the architect and the Moesian contractor appointed for the refurbishment work. The architect had subcontracted day-to-day contract administration to a local firm, and an effort was made to tighten up procedures in order to nip problems in the bud, but this was not really as effective as it needed to be. The result was a growing list of defective works to be put right, and an increasing time delay. Worst of all, some of the long-lead imported items, such as prefabricated aluminium extrusions for shopfitting applications, had been spoilt by careless handling, and would have to be either reordered or tolerated in an imperfect state.

The architect, in his reports to the board, was inclined to present this as the contractor's problem, but as time went on, it became increasingly obvious that it was a problem to all, wherever the contractual responsibility lay. These issues also caused a marked deterioration in relations between Group B's Western consultants and the local contractors. Local consultants acting between the two had an unexpected task of diplomacy on their hands, which became increasingly difficult to manage; the contractors saw the demands of the consultants as stiff and unreasonable, and the consultants saw the contractors as feckless. Mutual respect was gone, and talk of enforcement of the contract conditions on the increase. Group B, alarmed by this rapid deterioration in relations, and its possible implications for the longer-term project, took a stern attitude with its professional representatives, and made it clear that only a good and timely result was acceptable.

At the same time, the training programme of the railway staff was running into trouble. Top Trainers were well used to working abroad, but their previous experience was mainly in the countries of the Pacific Rim. It had not prepared them for the systems or the demotivation found in a former communist country. It has already been mentioned that standard state employment conditions made no allowance for training time within the working day: the employee's job was to be committed solely to his or her work throughout the working day, and the law was prescriptive of how the contracted hours should be spent. In other words, the system measured commitment of resources, not productivity. Also, the workforce was very suspicious of the initiative, and unwilling to put in additional time for no pay; to them, it appeared to be a conspiracy to defraud them of their own time, badly needed for other things.

In a situation of impasse, with an inflexible employment law on the one hand and a lack of resources in the appropriate part of the state budget to pay overtime on the other, it became obvious that it was expected of Group B as the moneyed party to pay overtime to the trainees.

This was agreed as a way out of a problem that was becoming chronic, but not without misgivings that an unfortunate precedent might be set. Indeed, the fears were compounded by other doubts, when it became apparent that pay bought the attendance of the delegated staff, but not their concentration or commitment. 'Work is a place we go to', said one of the managers, ironically.

Strategic planning of the redevelopment

In the meantime, the professional teams for the redevelopment of the railway land had been assembled. The poor experience of dealing with Moesian consultants in the refurbishment works (they had seemed out of date in design matters, and ineffectual in dealing with contractual problems) caused Group B to consolidate with known, high-quality design consultants from the West for this work. It was agreed, though, that team composition would be reviewed at the end of work stage D (scheme design).

The scheme which emerged was much liked within Group B, and received favourable comment in the architectural press. An enlightened plan for implementation, based on construction management, with packages of work sourced from local or foreign contractors or suppliers, was thought to provide an excellent balance of the economies possible from local levels of cost with the high levels of performance which could only be achieved with contractors used to the levels of expectation in the West, and with the skills to work accordingly. These strands were to be married together by a high-profile, rigorous project manager who 'spoke the client's language'.

WHO IS THE CLIENT?

All this was agreed with the government and local government bodies. It was only much later, years after the event, that it emerged in a casual conversation that the phrase 'spoke the client's language' had been completely misunderstood by half the people present at the strategy meeting. The Moesian representatives had thought that it referred to them, as the majority shareholder and host to the project. In fact, it was intended by Group B to refer to their own camp, as the prime movers of the project, not only in terms of linguistics, but also work culture. This misunderstanding was the root of much bad feeling, in which each side came to the conclusion that the other was untrustworthy and unrealistic.

TEAM STRUCTURE IN THE DETAILED DESIGN AND PRODUCTION INFORMATION STAGES

Given the chosen method of procurement, it was to be expected that a dialogue would begin fairly early in the progress of the work stage. This turned out only to be partly the case.

The design team members got on well together. The architect and structural engineer had worked together before, and understood each other's way of working with little difficulty. The mechanical and electrical engineer was adaptable, and, having good links with contracting organizations as well as a high level of design competence, was able to provide thought-through, practical solutions to difficult problems with fluency.

The team identified the areas of work where Western expertise was required. A lot of these were supply items, and in some cases supply and fix where special skills or understanding of systems was required. Where a Western manufacturer had a local agent, it was the policy to work through the agent and nominate his preferred specialist for labour.

However, although good, steady progress was made with negotiations on familiar territory in the West, progress locally varied from meteoric, with a complete subjugation of problems arising in negotiation, to extremely slow, with little understanding demonstrated at all of what was required.

Both situations began to cause some disquiet. The more cautious members of the team began to show a preference for using more Western contractors, particularly the mechanical and electrical engineer, whose work method depended on a close relationship with the contracting side.

This situation produced dislocation of the programme, with a number of items on the critical path becoming increasingly out of kilter.

SUSPENSION OF THE TRAINING PROGRAMME

These anxieties were compounded by the recommendation of Top Trainers that the training programme be suspended for the time being.

The problem of attendance, cured to some extent by payment of overtime out of Group B's budget, had been replaced by a blatant attitude of disengagement and boredom by the trainees. It was apparent that the training was seen as irrelevant and even comical by the middle-level staff. Appeals to the higher levels of management (who tended not to attend their own training sessions in any number) had little effect, one manager actually saying that it was Top Trainers' problem, and he should not be bothered with it.

Top Trainers approached the problem in a professional way, and tried a number of approaches to overcome it; but they reached the conclusion that if they remained an outside initiative, with no base of support either amongst the workforce or in the management echelon, they were wasting time and resources.

For Group B, this was an embarrassing setback.

THE REFURBISHMENT CONTRACT

A further crisis was reported when the local consultant reported that practical completion had been reached. The architect, not believing that the raft of quality problems had really been overcome, made a site visit, and found that the situation was as bad as ever. Finding the

141

attitude of the local consultant who had been administering the contract incredible in suggesting that practical completion had really been achieved, he demanded an explanation. The local man shrugged, and said 'What can one do? This is Moesia.' Furious at what seemed like a complete abandonment of the standards they had been working for, he sacked the local consultant on the spot.

This, of course, immediately created a new problem: how to get the contract finished, and how to get the message about standards across to the contractor. The situation was gloomy: delays and extra cost seemed inevitable. Negotiations made little progress. It appeared that a change of contractor as well as consultant was more or less unavoidable.

At this point, the station master mentioned privately to Muine Dischis (the interpreter/local manager) that his brother had a contracting firm that worked abroad, mainly in Germany and Austria, doing contract jobs, some of it shopfitting and exhibition work. He said that it was possible that his brother might come back for Easter, and be prepared to work for a few weeks with his men to finish the job off.

The architect was very dubious about this. Apart from anything else, it seemed to be an impossible situation to broke with Group B, which was certainly not used to unofficial solutions of this sort. Muine Dischis, whose local networking skills were considerable, took a different view, and encouraged him to go to Frankfurt to meet the brother, Gheorghe Cauciuc.

Out of desperation, he went, and met Mr Cauciuc at the Frankfurt International Book Fair, where his firm, Moescon, was one of five approved contractors for fitting out stands and other temporary structures. It was immediately clear that Moescon was a successful company which knew about meeting the expectations of Westerners. The architect put up in a hotel, and sent for the quantity surveyor to come from Paris.

It was apparent that salvation could be bought, but at a price. Moescon's success lay in being able to beat Westerners on price on their own territory, through having a lower cost base. Transfer them to Moesia, and their pricing levels were higher than average – higher, in fact, than any of the contractors who had tendered for the refurbishment contract. This was partly because they had established a rate of profit and of tradesmen's pay which was much above Moesian levels, but also because they expected to do a better job, were not overeconomical with materials and built in a margin for managing problems without losing time.

The architect reported back to his board, and after argument and some recrimination, it was agreed that there was no choice, and the

Key issues: training project — ownership of the idea

The railway managers had agreed to the project, but had not understood or committed themselves to what it meant. The culture of the organization steamed on, unchanged. For that reason, the demands of the training programme became resented not only by the trainees, but also by the managers, as it became just one more thorn in their flesh.

A large-scale training programme, the desired outcome of which is a fundamentally different approach to customers, embodies a shift of emphasis in the organization as a whole. It is certain to involve more effort, more cost and more problems in the short term. To a beleaguered organization in a difficult economic situation, all these may be extremely unwelcome.

Nevertheless, it is vital to get full support from the management echelon, expressed to the workforce and, in due course, to the public. The workforce needs to understand the benefit, and see that a better railway means better jobs.

All of this is very difficult in a subdivision of a large, nationalized organization, hemmed in with restrictive legislation. In the culture of blame for rule-breaking, which is the heritage of all postcommunist states, it is asking too much of managers to go out on a limb and make exceptions, unless there is sanction from above for them to do so.

The Berzozil pilot project needed to be constituted accordingly. Its senior staff needed to become an incorporated part of the project, and advocates of its benefits. Their actions and style needed to be representative of its values. Without this, the whole issue became doubtful.

This can be generalized to the project generally. Parties left on the fringe, unless motivated by their own professionalism, can all too easily diverge from the common objective. Ownership of the common objective means ownership of its standards, and commitment to its success. In the case of the refurbishment project, contractors were expected, within a predetermined timescale, to attain standards outside their normal range, not mutually established in advance, but imposed by a visiting outsider. In order to have any hope of meeting this challenge, they needed a leader who understood the achievability of the aims, as well as the expectations of the customer. This person was eventually found, in the person of Gheorghe Cauciuc.

priority lay with bringing the refurbishment to a conclusion that left a satisfactory physical result in place for all to see.

RADICAL RETHINKS

Following this, the refurbishment was completed successfully, to a reasonable standard of finish, showing rough edges only here and there where the new work had not quite obliterated the mistakes of the first contract. The reconstituted marble tiles of the booking hall, for instance, were set slightly off alignment with the main front wall, giving an untidy edge detail. A mistake in the setting out of the WC drainage connections meant that the WC cubicles were of rather widely varying size, which the modular cubicle construction was unable to mask satisfactorily.

Nevertheless, the work was done more or less on time, and Gheorghe Cauciuc's men had met their brief. Their performance was a bright spark in an otherwise gloomy scene.

The official ceremony marking the completion of the refurbishment works had the makings of a very tense event. The traditional Moesian way of making the most of a party saved the occasion, but it could not repair the tensions, dented egos and dismissive attitudes of criticism which had built up between the parties. Only two characters moved easily in the landscape of conflict: the interpreter/manager, Muine, and the replacement contractor, Gheorghe Cauciuc.

Group B returned to its London base aware that there were lessons in the refurbishment contract and the training programme which must be learnt, or the whole project might fail in a much bigger, more expensive and embarrassing way.

Discussions led nowhere much for a while, and the atmosphere of gloom intensified. The refurbishment contract had been saved through identifying and working with one key individual — Gheorghe Cauciuc; but the project as a whole was far too big to be addressed in such a way, and the whole experience of dealing with Moesian organizations and organization men was disastrously bad.

At this time, another cause of dislocation appeared. Changes in the top management of the railway at national level, following a corruption scandal, created further complications as the new directors set about moving their own nominees into subordinate management positions at county and district level.

It was Top Trainers who suggested that this upheaval was an opportunity for making a new start with the project structure, and incorporating the railway hierarchy into the matrix of the project in a much more complete way. The board agreed that this was certainly desirable, but what incentives could possibly be offered to make it stick?

The time of the annual Moesian International Trade Fair was approaching, and it was agreed that the architect's models of the redevelopment of the railway land, entitled 'Berzozil 2000', would be displayed prominently as an emblem of national progress, in the domed central hall of the exhibition centre. The building would include other key exhibits, such as the new model of Indonesian car now being assembled in a former armaments factory in the capital, and the full range of products of the American cosmetics factory recently established in the west of the country. Traditional Moesian produce would figure, as well.

Group B was holding one of its scheduled board meetings in Moesia to discuss this, and had asked Gheorghe Cauciuc to attend, because of his experience in exhibition work. Before he came into the room, Muine had suggested that he be made a member of the core team. 'I think he would like to have this status', she said, 'and he can help you'. This suggestion was supported by the Top Trainers director present, and was agreed.

The opportunity to promote Berzozil 2000 was clearly an important one, and there was a long discussion on how to maximize it. The structural engineer, whose gloomily cynical remarks had long ago earned him the nickname 'Eeyore', said that there was not much point in maximizing the prospect if it was not actually realizable. This raised the question once again of the lack of commitment shown by the local partner. Someone suggested that the exhibition include the local partner in a very positive way through the title 'CFM 2000 — A Railway Integrated with the Future'. The Berzozil project would illustrate this.

As this was no more than a restatement of the original, half-forgotten aims, it was agreed.

The new Director-General of CFM liked the idea of his railway forming the centrepiece of the exhibition. He also liked the thought of being 'integrated with the future'. The presentation Group B put forward included some sketch proposals for a logo and two posters, centred around this theme. The logo replaced the old, unmistakably communist emblem dating from the 1950s with a spare, elegant monogram. The posters showed a streamlined train passing through a modern office landscape. He asked if his office and the corporate headquarters entrance lobby could be refitted in this style, making use of the monogram.

Key issues

This scenario is one of cultural evolution, as well as cultural diversity of such breadth and depth that it is very hard to manage successfully and without conflict. It is a project only for the very skilful, and the brave.

The 'dirty washing' of such projects is rarely done in public, and the failures appear to the outside world mainly as delays and cost overruns, with an associated implication of management incompetence.

Incompetence may well be a justified charge, if the project concept did not include means for identifying and coping with the risks; in this case, it is clear that the risks were not understood initially, and that the project team as originally conceived was incapable of mastering the situation. It required the adoption of an individual, Gheorghe Cauciuc, and his organization, to get a grip on the situation. In this, it was not only the background of Cauciuc which was important, but also his personal capability and charisma. The success of the project revolved around his skills, and the human insight of Top Trainers, more than any other factor.

The temptation to send in the decorators at once was almost overwhelming, but the Paris-based quantity surveyor, who was present at the time of the request being made, made a measured reply. 'With the emblem goes also the action', he said, which fortunately translates into Moesian rather better than it does into English.

The upshot was that a PR campaign was quickly put together, linking the new image with the concepts of customer-centring, and modern commercial developments built around the railway. The Director-General appeared personally in some of the advertisements, and in more than a few television programmes, promoting the new vision.

He was also persuaded to make a regional tour timed to allow his presence at one of the staff training courses. This effectively forced the local directors to deliver an equivalent endorsement by attending themselves. The issue of staff uniforms to a new design was linked to the training programme.

At this stage, it was decided to overhaul the project structure. What emerged was a consolidated railway project board, with equal numbers from Group B and CFM. This had delegated authority from the Moesian Ministry of Transport and CFM (an unprecedented move in Moesia) and thus considerable agility by previous standards.

Acting under a licence from this body was Group B's development arm. This had effectively delegated its operational activities to a project management team, with instructions to put together construction packages in a form of construction management procurement. This decision was taken in order to compartmentalize skills and to give the best possible opportunity to manage performance and avoid the traps which had been exhibited in the refurbishment contract.

10

Case study: Alminster Old Town Hall

This is an imaginary case study. The issues raised in it are fictional, and no resemblance to any real situation is intended, nor are the events, people or organizations involved intended to represent real ones. However, photographs of an actual building, Warminster Town Hall, are used to give an idea of the appearance of the fictitious Alminster Town Hall

THE SITUATION

Alminster in Wiltshire is a market town lying just to the west of Salisbury Plain. Once prosperous, it is now rather run down; increasing mobility has caused the rural population to make Bath and Salisbury their preferred shopping destinations, and Alminster's importance as a local centre has declined. It remains, though, the one of the nearest towns to the army camps on Salisbury Plain, and the local shops and pubs are underpinned by the trade arising from their presence.

Alminster's high street visibly reflects the state of economic decline. By the normal standards of prosperous southern England, it seems like a fugitive from the 1970s. Plastic shop fascias, gappy displays in estate agents' windows, and pubs with bleak interiors and tired furniture all add to the impression of a place which has somehow failed to make it.

Yet Alminster is situated in desirable countryside, has good road and rail communications and has attractive stone buildings. Whilst it would never rival Salisbury or Bath for scope, given some economic

Alminster — main street

underpinning from modern light industry or commerce, it should be a good secondary centre. Prosperity has eluded it, but it must have been a near miss. There is always the feeling that the position should be capable of correction.

The high street consists of shops and houses. There is no established commercial area, and so far as there are offices they tend to be in upper floors over shops, or in a former residential building. The one recent development is the creation of a shopping arcade in a former narrow lane or mews opening directly off the high street. This is characterful, and works well.

Built in 1832, Alminster Town Hall was designed by Sir Edward Downs as a replica of a Jacobean country house, complete with coats of arms, but with only two storeys over a basement, rather than three. It is a classic statement of Victorian civic pride. Neat and comparatively small, it is a pleasing building to the eye, and is right in the heart of the town. It is listed Grade 2. It lost its original function in 1979, when it was superseded by a new building on an out-of-town site. Home to the magistrate's court for a while, it is now empty and has been in the hands of the Receiver. Even its neglected state, it is still the most conspicuous

Town hall — front

Town hall — side/rear

Town hall — derelict interior

and splendid building in the high street. Standing on a street corner, completely filling its site, its magnificence is only slightly diminished by the public lavatory and single-storey motor accessory shop immediately to its rear.

The layout of the building has two rooms at the front, and a single very large room at the rear of both the ground and the first-floor levels (these are the former courtrooms). The basement is a vaulted structure of considerable character, having been built as the town prison. It is fitted out as a wine bar.

The building has been deteriorating fast, although the masonry structure is still sound. The local council is concerned about the situation, and would welcome ideas for a new use.

The question is, what use? A number of organizations have looked at the site, but none so far has carried through a development plan. Perhaps this is because it is hard to make it fit either the rules or the conventional expectations for any set category of building. Car parking has

151

repeatedly been a stumbling block, as there is no space for parking on the site. Now the council has indicated that it would relax the requirements of its structure plan in this respect, in the interests of seeing a viable use generated for the building.

There is a repair grant scheme for the exterior of listed buildings, for which this building is eligible. The council's total annual allocation for this is £40 000.

THE PROJECT

Scene 1

A development company has recently acquired the building from the Receiver. For a period of several years before this, the building had been on the market, without finding a buyer.

With the building came some survey drawings and a sketch scheme for a leisure centre with two small cinema screens and ancillary accommodation. The existing wine bar in the basement is shown as retained in the scheme.

The development company, Foxglove Investments, has appointed a project manager from within its own staff, who is expected in turn to employ a team of external consultants representing a range of professional skills. It has asked for the existing sketch scheme to be reviewed, and for a viable strategic plan for enacting it. The scheme is to be modified as necessary to suit the perceived realities of the situation, and to maximize the site. There is to be a start on site without undue delay.

Key issues: exercise 1

Putting yourself in the position of the appointed project manager, decide on the skills required to make your team effective in these circumstances, and present this with a supporting rationale, and an outline programme.

Scene 2

The project has started briskly. Scheme designs are well under way, and the designers have begun to consider the construction and maintenance risks to workers and the public as required by the CDM Regulations.

The *Alminster Bugle* last Saturday had its front page dominated by the headline 'Town Hall in £1M Do-Up Deal', and a long article to the effect that the Town Hall has been bought by a development company, and is to be restored to its former glory and used as a leisure centre. The Mayor of Alminster, Cllr Bunce, was reported as saying that 'this is a great day for historic Alminster and for free enterprise'. Mention was made of the fact that grant assistance of the restoration from local authority funds was expected. Mrs Shona O'Hagan, a local resident, interviewed in the 'Occasions' coffee lounge, said 'It's a beautiful building and it's a disgrace that they let it get so bad and full of pigeons and dry rot and what not.'

The Alminster Trust (a very active pressure group) was asked by the newspaper for comment, but declined.

The planning department, as expected, has welcomed the news in principle, subject, of course, to public consultation and normal processes. In a planning consultation meeting it emerged that fairly recently there had been suggestions that the Town Hall be restored for use once again as the civic HQ of the council, with money from the National Lottery or the Millennium Fund. The planning officer stated in conversation that he thought that concept unrealistic.

You have now submitted your scheme to the planning department for initial comments. The drawings have been displayed in the council offices and attracted a lot of interest. Lobbying has already begun; it is clear that the shopkeepers in the arcade are unhappy about the possibilities both of competition and of the present parking facilities being used and perhaps dominated by users of the restored building.

A favourable response has come from the nearby army camp on Salisbury Plain. The adjutant has said that there is a great need for a place for 'the chaps to get a night out'. This causes some wry remarks amongst the locals; most of the pubs in Alminster have banned the army as too boisterous and inclined to pick fights.

A preliminary site meeting with the building inspector has brought up the issue of the soundness of the existing structure. He is unhappy about your proposal to take bearing off the existing walls, and asks for justification of their load-bearing capacity and that of the foundations. It is clear that he would prefer to see a new independent structure within the building, but has no suggestions as to how this should be made compatible with the existing vaulting in the basement.

Questions are also being asked about means of escape in case of fire.

Your board of directors is very keen to have the building air-conditioned. The managing director has a water–water heat pump in his home, and says that it's marvellous. When the site investigation reveals that there is a canalized brook under the building, he encourages the board to insist on a reverse-cycle heat pump system to heat and cool the building.

Key issues: exercise 2

Consider how these occurrences, and their implications, affect your project; how to deal with the technical aspects, and how to manage conflict. Identify the needs of other stakeholders, and how they may be accommodated. Develop strategies for dealing with the possible contingencies.

Scene 3

Shock. The local authority has issued a repairs notice, requiring the Town Hall as a listed building to be put back into good original condition immediately. When you ring up the planning department, you are told that this is a legitimate statutory requirement, and the only reason it has not been issued previously is that there was no point serving the notice on the previous owner, who was bankrupt.

Further discussion reveals that the Notice has been insisted on by English Heritage, which is opposed to conversion of the building in principle, as it compromises its originality. It is clear that the local authority does not wholly agree with this, but has had to go along with it.

Nevertheless, relations with the local planners remain good, and you are able to agree in principle a mansard roof, providing that there is no rooftop plant. They have also confirmed the eligibility of the building for a discretionary repairs grant. One of the rules of the grant is that no work may begin until the grant is finalized.

Wessex Water has refused permission for a groundwater source for the heat pump, but has not said why.

The Alminster Trust has now embarked on a campaign for restoration of the Town Hall 'for community use', and the matter has begun to appear frequently in the *Alminster Bugle*. It is not clear how the Trust would be able to carry any scheme out, but they are clearly articulate and in a position to do a lot of harm. Today, there was a front-page article in the *Bugle*, which made much of the fact that a non-executive director of your company is a distant relative of Robert Maxwell. The headline was 'Stop These Rapists — Give Us Back Our Town Hall'.

One of your directors, finding this very frustrating, half-seriously suggests putting in a listed-building application to demolish the building 'to concentrate their minds'.

Amid this turmoil, your professional design team is focusing on the buildability of the scheme, and the health and safety issues implied in it. The architect is keen to see a 'design-led solution', but the directors have discouraged any excessive time spent in producing drawings until a viable way forward is identified.

The alterations to the building suggested so far include the following:

- a penthouse storey behind the existing parapets
- a complete rearrangement of the first and second floors at the rear of the building to accommodate the ramped auditoria for the cinemas
- preservation and picturesque restoration of the vaults in the basement (the former town prison cells)
- air conditioning, a water–water heat pump and associated plant.

As the building covers the site almost completely, and has busy streets on its two exposed sides, works access and storage of materials are an issue from the start. The lifting of materials and components is also fraught with implications. It is not likely to be easy to resolve these issues in a way which protects the safety of construction workers and the public, and also makes the site reasonably operable.

Key issues: exercise 3

How would you get your team to prioritize the issues and rank the possible solutions? Indeed, what are the key issues at the present, and what are the peripheral ones? What work is needed to give the strategic choices to be made a context, and what is needed to illustrate and even 'sell' the possible solutions?

Consider the implications of:

- revised structural arrangements
- plant location and support
- measures to protect the public, including traffic
- exclusion of unauthorized persons
- unloading and loading
- rubbish removal.

Develop a strategy based on risk analysis, and provide a summary feedback to the design team.

Scene 4

In your office, there is an increasing realization that this project has started from a confused premise. The instructions were to take the existing scheme and modify it as necessary to achieve viability, but what does this actually mean? Against what is viability measured? There are no trade comparators to hand, and it is beyond the experience of your team to forecast cash flow in a series of 'what if' scenarios which really must depend on highly specialized input.

 You decide to stop, and reconsider the options, starting at first principles.

Key issues: exercise 4

With the benefit of hindsight, how should the client's business case be represented in the project strategy, and how should the team be configured to take account of this?

11

Case study: the Ark, Hammersmith, London W6

Commissioning client:	*Ake Larson*
Architect:	*Ralph Erskine with Rock Townshend and Lennart Bergstrom Architects*
Architect for fit-out:	*Marshall Cummings Marsh*
Structural engineer:	*Scandiaconsult AB, Andrew Kent & Stone*
Services engineers:	*Scandiaconsult AB, Dale & Goldfinger, Gosta Sjolander AB*
Construction managers:	*Ake Larsen*
Occupier:	*Seagram Distillers*
Floor area:	*17 000 m^2 (gross internal)*

The Ark is a truly extraordinary building: extraordinary not just to look at, but also in the design philosophy which formed it as a place to spend time, as an interactive work environment. That this should have been attempted on a small, blighted and noisy site, and that a very expensive building should have resulted, is even more surprising.

The Ark is a building commissioned by a contractor committed to enlightened forms of working; one form of enlightenment has begotten another. In the process, financial problems were encountered, which mean that the Ark is now in other hands.

INTRODUCTION: THE ARK AS ARCHITECTURE

True Functionalism is a superior work method, not a style
Ralph Erskine

The Ark is controversial; it is also a logical answer to a design problem. Behind the drama there is reason, but there is an insistent demand for attention. Like other notable, unconventional structures such as the Lloyds building in the City of London (Richard Rogers & Partners, 1986), the Willis Faber & Dumas building in Ipswich (Foster Associates, 1974) and the Renault headquarters in Swindon (Norman Foster Associates, 1983), it was commissioned by a client who wished to make a statement about his own organization. Interestingly, the present occupier of the building, Seagram, is similarly minded: it has previously commissioned a celebrated modern-movement skyscraper for its New York headquarters (Seagram building: Mies van der Rohe & Philip Johnson, 1956–8).

Ake Larson and Pronator, a Swedish firm of construction managers, acquired the site as a vacant lot in 1987, and approached Erskine to design a charismatic building. His first reaction was to decline the job, on the basis that the site was inhuman, and had no context to form a springboard for the design. However, in the end he took the commission: he was prevailed on, apparently, because of his close personal relationship with Ake Larson himself, and his respect for the company's vision and working methods.

Ake Larson is known in this country for innovative, fee-based construction management. The company's boast is that it 'sits on the same side of the table' as the client, and works closely with the client to achieve goals of quality and suitability as well as value. The management method involves an open book so far as costs are concerned, and a fee structure designed to ensure that adequate management resources are provided at all times.

Cultural forces underlying the composition

Ralph Erskine is said to have conceived the Ark as a medieval landscape (Singmaster, 1996). He described how the Ark's funnel shape grew from a wish to create a forum internally, a space where people would interact in the course of their work: 'My first sketches showed the funnel-shaped interior space, a cockpit for intensive social interaction'.

Perhaps more significantly, the Ark is clearly a shelter in a spot which is victim to the disturbance of traffic (at two levels), railway trains and an unsightly outlook. The Ark, though, does much to create its own environment: its hollow form encloses space, protects it and creates its own internal views; it is an oasis.

Erskine produced the concept, but it was worked up and detailed by Rock Townshend and Lennart Bergstrom. Rock Townshend had previously done a feasibility study for the site, but more importantly they 'had pioneered the concept of democratic workspace in Britain, and were fully in accord with the Erskine philosophy, as were Bergstrom' (Pearman, 1993).

SITING

Previously a car pound, the site is by all normal standards a blighted one: to the north is the Talgarth Road, the main artery to the west, which feeds the M4. Immediately to the north-west of the building, this rises up to form the Hammersmith Flyover, which not only is a considerable bulk but also projects traffic noise at a high level. Beyond the flyover, the top half of St Paul's Church is visible, equally blighted by its context, and marooned by the road system. The recently completed, postmodern Hammersmith Broadway development sits solidly in the middle distance.

Across the Talgarth Road to the north is the Novotel hotel building, a 13-storey, sheer-sided structure of the 1970s.

Wrapping round the building, from north-west to east-south-east, is the London Underground railway, four tracks wide, in a shallow cut. This is again a generator of considerable noise, which, as things turned out, the sloping faces of Erskine's building were to magnify annoyingly.

Beyond the tracks lies an area of Edwardian, brick-built terrace housing, in streets which are remarkably peaceful, considering the near proximity of so many potential sources of disturbance. The backs of the houses on the north side of Yeldham Road bear the brunt of the noise from the railway, of course, but otherwise the main impact of the world outside is the strange profile of the Ark's rooftop superstructures, peering over the regular roofline of the terrace.

EXTERNAL FORM

Critics struggle to find an evocative epithet for the Ark's extraordinary shape. An egg, a beehive, a barrel and a stranded spaceship all help give colour to an explanation, but Ark is the best name, tying together the strands of a hull form and an enclosure or sanctuary from the hostile environment outside. (Its origin as a name for the building is unclear; it may originally have been just a pun on Ake Larsen.)

The hull form on props, like a ship on the slipway, is as arresting as a building form can be; the Ark is unmistakable, a sculptural landmark of the west of the city, as Tower Bridge is of the east.

The impact on which this effect relies is a function of form and size. The Ark is a surprising, big, round thing, close — daringly close — to the raised highway. It is outrageous, it flouts the polite vocabulary of urban

The Ark (sketch by Ralph Erskine)

The Ark — exterior view across the London Underground railway tracks (copyright Chris Gascoigne/Arcaid)

composition and looks as though it was designed to shock more than to please. It gets your attention, all right, but you might not like it at first. The crazy skyline looks deliberately contrived, an almost naive assembly of components at funny angles, the function of which is doubtful. The roof does not quite seem to fit, and everything is terribly brown. Is this actually a considered design, or just an exercise in throwing the rule book as far away as possible? Is it real high tech, or just a fashion victim, strapped about with a load of gizmos? And what kind of a design solution is it, anyway, that forces such a large structure into this small desolate spot?

The last question knocks at the foundations of the concept. The site is blighted, apparently good for nothing except the most humdrum of utilitarian uses, such as the car pound it used to be. One thinks of Portakabins and sheds as the likely building form on such a bit of space-left-over-after-planning. No doubt the site was relatively cheap, and in the euphoria of the late 1980s property boom, it probably looked like a bargain route to a presence in the western fringes of central London.

The building, seen from the ground, appears to be oval in plan, but this is not the case: it fills the site by being an asymmetric, but near-equilateral triangle, with the corners rounded off on a large radius. The site has been maximized relentlessly, and it is the inward taper of the elevations down towards the ground which generates a little space about the building; without it, the plot ratio would be almost 100%.

STRUCTURE

The Ark is a steel-framed building, unusual in the cantilevering required as a consequence of its tapering form. The floors are constructed on the 'slim-floor' system, which is a cousin to filler-joist construction, in that the steel beams lie within, rather than beneath, the concrete slab thickness. Basically, this system consists of precast slabs supported on the lower flange of a top-hat section, or, less frequently, a universal column section. The latter was used at the Ark, in conjunction with slabs chamfered on their top edge to clear the upper flange of the universal column. Floor sections with a curved outer edge were cast *in situ*, with a rolled steel channel as permanent edge shuttering. From the sixth floor up, the slabs are hung at the edge by columns which act in tension.

PLANNING

The Ark is a building whose form follows its function, most of the time. But when we look critically at the primary aspects of layout, the logic slips.

Although the site has been maximized, the size of individual floors is relatively small; too small to accommodate a typical department in any organization that might occupy the whole building. Scrutiny reveals that this is a product of the relatively small footprint of the building, and of floor space sacrificed to the atrium. The form of the building has therefore followed some notions of function, but not the need to accommodate certain numbers in groups of a critical mass. Interestingly, the same is true of Centre Point, another landmark building, in which a slim tower produced small individual floor areas.

This fault certainly limited the appeal of both buildings to potential occupiers, and is given as a reason for the relatively long period taken to let them (although there were other factors as well in the case of Centre Point). The defence is, in the case of the Ark, that rigid divisions of territory are unnecessary, because communication between spaces is so good. This is an answer that can only be preached to the converted; to most organizations, it merely amounts to a failure to cater for their needs. This must be counted a significant flaw in a commercial building. Otherwise, though, the layout never ceases to surprise and delight. As one moves through the Ark, there is an impression of space opening out around and above, which is hard to parallel in any other building. The atrium dominates the interior. It floods it with light, and creates a sense of a greater enclosure — that is to say, the enclosure of the space beyond the area immediately around one. It is all too easy to feel exposed and uncomfortable when sitting in large spaces, but not here. Erskine has played the game of scale and volume masterfully, and exploited it in every way.

In the Globe Theatre, an actor at the centre can direct communication hither and thither, and the audience can participate; similarly, in the Ark, individuals can be seen at their workstations, or moving about, above or below. Meetings take place in a vantage point with a hemispherical skeleton dome, so visitors are reminded throughout their time in the building of being amid action, in a space enclosed by a space — a situation emphasized by the wall climber lifts moving up and down within the atrium.

Brilliant the Ark may be, but it is not perfect. Some spaces, including the meeting places, such as the skeleton-domed vantage point and the 'crow's nest' above roof level are on the small side, and it is hard to make visual presentations in them because of the amount of natural light. There is a constant risk of disturbance of one area by another, and particularly by those moving about the building. Seagram's staff police their own movements, and avoid passing the open meeting rooms when they are in use.

INTERNAL ENVIRONMENT

Any building which has a huge, nine-storey-high atrium, not separated from the working floors, and lit by a vast south-facing composite window, has to provoke scepticism about its environmental

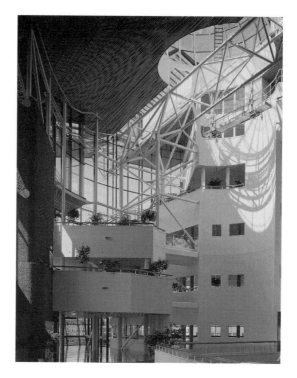

The Ark — interior view: the atrium (copyright Chris Gascoigne/Arcaid)

performance. The Ark, with all these features, is a triumph of climate control. It is a comfortable, airy, sunny building.

The Ark is a triple-glazed, sealed building, because of the sources of noise nuisance and pollution which surround it. The atrium's enormous, south-facing glazed wall is protected by solar louvres and roof overhang to minimize the intrusion of high-angle sunlight. Nevertheless, the thermal dynamics of the atrium must operate on a large scale in extreme weather. The success of the environmental system has to be ascribed to the comprehensive way in which its elements interact to create a balance.

THE BUILDING IN USE

Asked what the building was like from a user's point of view, a Seagram employee emphatically responded 'wonderful'. Others were similarly enthusiastic, so the appeal of the building has the depth to withstand familiarity. It is a building of which its occupiers are proud, and they feel that it works well. Perhaps the truth is that it works well in sympathetic hands. As Martin Frost, president of Seagram Europe and Africa said:

> Choosing the Ark was based on a number of factors: outstanding design and space in the building, the convenience of the location, the opportunity to create an open working culture.

Key issues

With the perspective of hindsight, the Ark project seems holistic in the extreme, in that everything from procurement method to use is combined under a single philosophy.

Whether or not this assessment is truly accurate, it forms a useful basis for considering in a reconstructive way the strategic options which define the track of any construction project which has an end use in mind.

Ake Larson, as a firm of construction managers, was in a position to dictate with authority the procurement method as well as the configuration of the building. It could be argued that events proved it faulty in both departments:

- the firm was unable to complete the building itself, because of its complexity, and the firm's financial overcommitment
- once completed, the Ark proved difficult to let.

The vision was of a building, its users and its procurement, but financiers restrict their view to viability, and purchasers of office space speak in terms of location, area and servicing, without necessarily giving much weight to the priorities demonstrated in the Ark. These latter people would have been looking for a unity of another sort – the unity of product identity with market.

It could be argued therefore, that the Ark probably ignored in its concept some of the important stakeholders on which its viability depended. Of course, those stakeholders would have seemed less important at time the key decisions were taken: economic recessions have effects which are often not foreseen; radicalism can turn out to be unexpectedly expensive. With the blinding clarity of hindsight, it is all too easy to be critical. Yet it seems that the singleness of purpose which made the building unique also interfered with its commercial viability.

Key issues: exercise

Put yourself in the position of the project manager and consider the following.

The Ark was conceived as *democratic workspace*, with its funnel-shaped interior a *medieval landscape* — but some would say that its form was mainly a response to the constraints of the site. In any case, it was finally let as a *landmark building*; in other words, the aesthetics of its appearance and interior planning were of very great importance, and compensated for other disadvantages. Could a viable project be planned on the basis of either premise? How, bearing in mind the diverse business needs of (a) the client as potential occupier and (b) the client as contractor–sponsor? What are the implications for the composition of the project team (including sponsors and any potential occupier) for either option?

If key members of the board (to which you report) are already convinced of their own vision, how should any contrary views be given worthwhile authority?

The vision has, of course, proved itself capable of being realized in every technical way, at a price. It is in fact a technical and aesthetic triumph, dearly bought. But the Ark was a very risky project undertaken at a dangerous time, on a difficult and marginal site. How could it have been procured (design and construction) in a way that made it less vulnerable?

Architects and other designers often complain that their contribution is made subservient to that of economists. In the Ark, it seems that the reverse was true. How is the balance to be struck in a project team?

FURTHER READING

Collymore, P. (1994). *The Architecture of Ralph Erskine*. Academy Editions, London.

Duffy, F. (1992). Office cultures. *Architect's Journal* **195**, No. 23, 28.

Egelius, M. (1990). *Ralph Erskine, Architect*. Byggforlaget/Swedish Museum of Architecture.

Erskine, R., Lennart Borgström Arkitektkontor and Rock Townsend (1992). Cladding, office. *Architect's Journal* **195**, No 23, 40.

Parkyn, N. (1992). Building the Ark: a Swedish approach. *Architect's Journal* **195**, No. 23, 46.

12

Case study: Argent House

This is an imaginary case study. The issues raised in it are fictional, and no resemblance to any real situation or property is intended, nor are the events, people or organizations involved intended to represent real ones.

The case study refers to work stages based on the RIBA Plan of Work.

SCENE 1

Mr Hugh Miller, a captain of industry, decided to move his home back to London after living in Oxfordshire for some years. He set out to get himself a dwelling of country house proportions, superbly equipped, surrounded by garden, within a few minutes' car journey of the centre of London.

This difficult objective was not to be achieved by buying a house already suitable for his purposes. Such few houses that came on the market were either fantastically expensive, or just not good enough. Mr Miller decided to build.

Mr Miller had been a client to a number of industrial building projects, and he had a knowledge of construction from his university education as a mechanical and electrical engineer. The idea of building, or substantially rebuilding, his own house was therefore not one which seemed unreasonable to contemplate. Also, he had an international reputation for knocking things into shape; an energetic manager, rather harsh toned and by no means a 'people person', his

Argent House — part of the conservatory

determination, energy and clarity of vision normally led to success. On the other hand, he was demanding, humourless and unloved.

Eventually, suitable raw material for the project was found, in the form of a Victorian villa with substantial gardens and views of a park. Listed Grade 2, it was on two floors over a semibasement, and built in an Italianate style, with a Lombard turret over the front entrance. In every detail, from the stone staircase to the slowly collapsing conservatory, it presented a picture of fading elegance. Predictably enough, although mainly structurally sound, it failed to measure up to the purchaser's specification in most respects.

Mr Miller employed an architect to carry out a study of the building, and examine how his needs could be met. These were simply set out as:

- Spacious and elegant drawing room, dining room and study; conservatory
- Kitchen, back kitchen, and utility room; walk-in safe
- Garage integrated into house
- Master suite with spacious bedroom with balcony, two attached bathrooms, and walk-in closet; informal sitting room, separate dressing room
- guest suite

- staff flat
- indoor swimming pool at least 13 m long with changing and shower room, plant room, etc.
- air conditioning
- high standard throughout.

No budget was set, but estimates were asked for.

Given that the house had eight bedrooms as existing, making a two-bedroom-plus staff flat within the space might not seem to be too difficult, and the architects were able to come up with a convincingly attractive and practical scheme. The problems, it was already obvious, were going to be with the swimming pool.

Not only was the existing envelope of the house a little small to fit the pool in comfortably, but a test hole had revealed the alarming presence of groundwater 600 mm below the basement floor, in a gravel stratum.

At this point, it was decided to appoint an engineer to review the ground conditions, and present options for the construction of the pool. The architects were also instructed to proceed with developing the scheme, and make initial proposals to the planners.

Key issues: exercise 1

What team structure would you like to see in place at this point?

How would you identify the need for a particular appointment, and the professional characteristics of the appointee? Do these flow from the brief? Do they relate to the character of the client?

SCENE 2

It became obvious that the best course of action to accommodate the swimming pool, given the difficult ground conditions, was going to involve demolition of half the house, creation of a deep basement within a new retaining structure, and subsequent rebuilding of the house. This was readily accepted by Mr Miller, and by the planning department, despite the listed-building status. It was also agreed that the rebuilt structure would be slightly deeper in plan than the existing one, making the planning of the rooms considerably better.

Fairly early on, a services consultant was appointed, and given a performance brief for the air-conditioning installation, involving a high degree of control for individual room temperatures. This developed into a design which was clearly going to be very expensive to implement. This was confirmed by estimates. After a fruitless period of discussion, in which the services consultant washed his hands of the problem on the basis that he had followed the brief set, Mr Miller asked the architect to dismiss the consultant. An argument over his fees ensued.

A replacement consultant, well known to the architect, was then appointed. This second consultant was given the job on the basis that he was used to working very closely with contractors, and his initial proposal was worked up jointly with the contractor who ultimately got the installation job. The design was simpler, but still met the broad objectives of the brief, and the estimate was at an acceptable level.

At the architect's suggestion at the start of the production information stage, a quantity surveyor was employed too, with the brief of writing a bill of quantities, making interim valuations and settling the final account.

Mr Miller made a point of frequently contacting each team member personally. He was a great one for ringing people up 'to find out how they were getting on'. He found this an effective way of keeping tabs on the problems and making it obvious to all that his job needed priority. It also tended to bring out the existence of problems at an early stage, although some said that this did not so much contribute to their early resolution, as to a sense of crisis.

There was a lot of pressure for an early start on site, but the complexity of the systems and finishes and the detailed demands of the client astonished everyone. It was not unusual for the architect to arrive in his office in the morning to find a dozen pages of fax with many detailed questions and requests for sketches to illustrate particular points. Because Mrs Miller could not visualize space, or read a technical drawing, every part of the building had to be drawn in 3D. This requirement, together with frequent changes of mind, made for slow progress, but the architect felt unable to question the method of working: he was stuck with it, he thought, and must make the best of it.

In order to accelerate things, he suggested that the building work be tackled in two stages: structural and fit-out. This idea was accepted, and the structural work, phase 1, was sent out to competitive tender, on the basis of the JCT 80 form of contract.

The tender documents included the structural engineer's scheme for a secant pile dam. This was a wall of bored piles filled with clay, intersected by bored concrete piles, to create a waterproof temporary structure. It was fully designed by the structural engineer, but the propping required to support this new structure whilst excavation was taking place within it, and the new basement structure was being cast, was not designed but was to be put forward by the contractor as part of his or her tender.

Two tenderers put in bids, the third having dropped out. One of the two ignored the secant pile dam design, and produced his own scheme based on sheet piling. The other priced the secant piling, but did not describe the temporary support scheme, which was 'to follow'.

This second tender was the one accepted. The first was discarded because the sheet-piling solution was thought impracticable so close to other structures and to boundaries — and also because the tenderer had not priced for the work asked for, which was thought improper and annoying.

Key issues: exercise 2

Do you agree with the way the job is being handled? What advice would you give Mr Miller about the team structure? Would you accept his demands as the architect did?

Are Mr Miller's expectations likely to be met by a traditional professional team in which no project manager plays a part? If one is needed, and Mr Miller is truly a project manager at heart, should he employ one, or do the job himself?

SCENE 3

The second contractor, Macarly Ltd, was appointed subject to the usual conditions and the provision of a programme and a method statement for the engineering works to the satisfaction of the structural engineer.

Work began on site, and initially excellent progress was made with the demolitions, excavations and piling works. In the meantime, work continued on detailed design and production information for the fit-out.

The structural engineer received Macarly's method statement and rejected it. A resubmission was also rejected.

At this point, the structural engineer made adverse comments on the attitude of the contractor to technical matters, and suggested that it would be a good idea to have a site engineer during the remainder of the groundworks phase. This was agreed.

Argent House — groundworks

The works of propping the pile dam and then excavating within it, between the piles, continued uneasily. Whilst the amount of propping was not in dispute, the measures need to adapt the propping, including temporary absences of support whilst machines were moved, proved very intractable. It appeared, as the architect commented privately, that the contractor was 'being asked to do the excavation with a teaspoon', in amongst a forest of props.

The presence of a site engineer, far from solving the problem, seemed to make the situation worse. Regarded by the contractor as a spy in the camp and an unnecessary brake on progress, and simultaneously by Alf, the site agent, as an inexperienced puppy who knew little of real construction, a situation of real personal conflict began to develop. Alf was in his mid sixties, cheerful and positive by nature, but not one to suffer fools gladly. He resented bitterly the imposition of petty rules on him in a situation where (to his mind) experience and *ad hoc* measures were the route to successful solving of the problems. Rows developed from day to day, and on one occasion, Alf told the site engineer to get out of his way, or he 'would give him one'. Apologies were demanded, conciliatory meetings were held, but permanent damage had been done.

Mr Miller, following his normal practice, networked constantly in the early stages, but progressively distanced himself from the problem, and began to restrict his calls to the architect and quantity surveyor.

The architect was worried about the situation, because it seemed to him that the engineer's scheme was unbuildable, or close to it. He had serious misgivings about the division of responsibility between permanent and temporary works, and suspected that the scheme had never been thought through so far as construction was concerned, either by the engineer or by the contractor. The site agent, Alf, confided to him that he thought the only way to get the main permanent members in was to remove some of the propping temporarily and put in the permanent members quickly, before the pile dam deflected.

Mr Miller, by now both frustrated and rather worried that Argent House might remain as an expensive hole in the ground for ever, told the architect that he expected him to sort the matter out.

Key issues: exercise 3

Who carries the responsibility for making this team successful? What is the required action?

SCENE 4

One morning, early, before the site engineer arrived on site, Alf took out the props, and put in a small machine to take out the rest of the spoil, replacing props after it as it went. He ignored the protests and forecasts of collapse of the excavation and surrounding structures, and cast in the first of the permanent ground beams. There was an almost audible sigh of relief that the vicious circle had been broken without incurring disaster.

However, if the contractor was expecting thanks for his initiative, he got none. The most favourable response was a lack of criticism. Some parties, particularly the structural engineer, were openly contemptuous of his 'gross irresponsibility'.

Mr Miller said little. His chauffeur-driven car arrived at the site most days, and he stalked around the muddy patch in his galoshes with an air of impatience, asking questions here and there.

However, as the building began to rise out of the ground, morale improved. The apparent progress once the bricklayers and carpenters

Key issues: exercise 4

There are some inherent problems here in the very nature of the client, and the team of consultants are in a no-win situation in trying to deal with the resultant situation.

How could this have been recognized in time, and strategies used to cope with it, before the present culture developed? Is it simply a situation of the architect needing to be firm at an early stage, and dictating the ground rules for decision, with a timetable? Or, if such a regimen would simply be unacceptable to a client who 'wants what he wants', is something more subtle required to manage the situation, without damaging 'us and them' splits occurring? Is the right form of procurement being used?

If, for instance, construction management were used, with a client's project manager heading the team, could the in-built difficulties be more effectively managed? Who should coordinate the client's wishes in the interior design?

were working was encouraging for all, and tension reduced — but old issues remained unforgiven.

A decision was made to move some outstanding work, including some of the less time-critical sections of brickwork, and part of the drainage system, to Phase 2. This was expressed as being in the interests of bringing an unhappy time to a close — but perhaps it was really more a matter of terminating an unhappy team.

Phase 2 started with a bang. The new contractor, Gross and Baldey, clearly had a much more effective management base, and far better logistical arrangements. Their paperwork was prompt and accurate. When they wanted information, they asked for it in a clear way, and made it obvious where they felt the boundaries of their responsibilities lay.

But after a while, problems of timing began to emerge. Because of Mrs Miller's fascination with each new idea, the interior design simply continued until it was fixed by being constructed, and then, if it did not accord exactly with her imagined expectation, it had to be changed. Similarly, decorative schemes became the subject of repetitive, long-drawn-out trial processes, in which the required result could not successfully be explained, but instead had to be demonstrated. Sample panel after sample panel was rejected, work on site had to be repeated, and the effect told in the contract programme.

This process proved uncontrollable. Although good manners dictated an approach of 'the client is always right', on the part of both the design team and the contractor, the disruptions became too great to be ignored. Claims for delay were mentioned, and angrily rejected by the client. The architect found his duty as contract administrator increasingly trying. Increasingly, he could not support his client with honesty, but was apprehensive of the consequences of too much disagreement, which might appear as disloyalty. As lead consultant he was identified for better or worse with the client and his wishes. Under the JCT contract and traditional form of procurement which was in use, he took the client's part in negotiations. But the simple system of allegiances which the contract engendered was put at risk by events.

13

Case study: Kelso Day Centre — a self-build scheme for the homeless in east London

This is an imaginary case study. The issues raised in it are fictional, and no resemblance to any real situation or property is intended, nor are the events, people or organizations involved intended to represent real ones.

THE CONTEXT

Stratney is a poor borough in the east of London. It has a large immigrant community, and unemployment is at levels exceeded in only one other London borough. Long-term unemployment is a particular problem, and high numbers of young people leave school only to become unemployed straight away, with little prospect of getting a job within a period of years.

THE ORIGINS OF THE PROJECT

Self-build projects were pioneered by Walter Segal, an architect. Since its beginnings in the 1960s, self-build has become a recognized means of creating needed facilities and morale-boosting activity simultaneously.

The initial idea

The Kelso Day Centre project was conceived by a group of local authority councillors and social services staff as a multifaceted project designed to:

- procure a needed social facility
- give ownership of the facility to elements of its target group, and thereby improve sense of ownership and reduce vandalism
- reduce costs in procurement
- develop skills and employability in a disadvantaged group
- provide temporary employment.

Many people within the local authority and the borough thought the plan much too idealistic, and therefore likely to fail. Its more sanguine supporters thought it less likely to fail in use, if it could be skilfully managed into existence.

The council was prevailed on to back the project, on the basis that:

(1) it made use of a site already owned by the council, which it had previously tried and failed to sell
(2) a project management proposal should be presented before initiation of any other expense, other than preliminary design sketches.

Desired outcomes

The council defined its desired outcomes in an unpublished minute in the following general way:

> Creation of opportunity for the Homeless in the construction and provision of a Day Centre for their use, with minimum cost risk to the Borough as Sponsor, good standards of Health & Safety and maximum effectiveness in the use of the resource of labour of homeless people.

A working group was set up to carry the matter forward.

Objectives

The working group recognized at an early stage that it lacked the expertise to define objectives in any detail. What, for instance, did 'maximum effectiveness in the use of the resource of labour of homeless people' actually mean in practical terms? Did it mean getting them to do as much as possible, or, on the other hand, getting them to do only the things that they were unlikely to spoil or have to do several times before an acceptable standard was achieved? If the answer was the first, how was the work to be supervised to minimize waste, and if the answer was the second, then how was training to be integrated into the project, in order to achieve one important aspect of the stated wish to create opportunity?

Research into the employer's responsibilities for health and safety, and in particular the CDM Regulations, revealed a nightmare of liability: young, undisciplined, unskilled people, let loose in a fundamentally risky environment, armed with tools they did not fully understand how to use, seemed a recipe for disaster and a negligence claim.

The working group therefore set about trying to identify:

(1) sources of expertise in such projects
(2) ways of the council devolving responsibility to those who could properly control the risks.

This proved to be quite difficult. Those who had experience of such projects nearly all were individuals rather than organizations, so no corporate body could be identified which was substantial enough to stand behind the project and shoulder the full burden of risk. The individual experts, although they were undoubtedly good at what they did, were all underqualified in an academic sense, or had moved away from their original subject, so proof of expertise had to rest solely on experience. One had been a marine engineer, another a warrant officer instructor in the Royal Engineers. Organizations which had the professional credentials to manage the project all lacked experience of its particular nature, and in any case could not afford to provide the service required at anything like an affordable cost.

There seemed to be an inescapable conflict in the brief: the use of the resource of the labour of homeless people was potentially impossible to manage safely, and also potentially impossible to align with any normal yardstick of cost-effectiveness. Perhaps the project was a non-starter.

At this point, the working group identified Peter Hackforth, a retired but highly regarded manager in this kind of project, who lived quite locally, and was willing to give advice. He refused to be co-opted to the group, however, since he 'could not stand committees'.

His formula had the following features:

(1) the establishment in advance of the project of a training facility with fairly rigorous selection of trainees for their potential

(2) the packaging of groundworks and all specialist trades such as electrical and plumbing work, to be let as direct contracts to specialist trade contractors.

The working group was dismayed. The purpose of the project was to benefit those who had been deselected by society, resulting in their becoming homeless. If they were now subjected to a process which deselected the majority of them once again, what had been achieved? And if the trainees were restricted to simple tasks, the achievement would seem very meagre, and the sense of ownership of the completed building might slip away.

Peter Hackforth told the group to 'get real'. You cannot expect a high percentage success rate from a group which is itself born, however unjustly, out of failure. If even 10% of the initial intake made it to the end of the project, that would be a good result. Some of the others would still benefit, even if they fell by the wayside. As for sense of ownership, he thought the criticism completely wrong. A contribution, however small, usually led to some sense of ownership, he said emphatically.

The working group, on reflection, accepted his views. There was then a move to abandon the new-build project in favour of a conversion job on a former laundry which was available, on the basis that this would use the limited skills available, without the need for nearly so much input by professional contractors.

In the end, the debate went another way, and the decision was made in principle to focus on a single-storey, timber-framed building on a raft foundation, with a mineral slate roof. The interior would be dry lined in a particularly damage-resistant firecheck board. This meant that the input by specialist trade contractors would be kept to a minimum, and the output by the student builders maximized.

PROJECT DEFINITION

The working group therefore came to define the project in two parts:

(1) the establishment of a training facility for homeless people in building skills, with a focus on carpentry and general work such as laying concrete slabs and screeds
(2) the development of the day centre project with design by those experienced in self-build schemes and construction in packages by

a limited number of trade specialists and by teams under instruction from the training facility.

This definition was accepted by the local authority and other, informally constituted, community groups.

DEVELOPING THE BRIEF AND DEFINING ROLES

'Base Camp 1 has been established', said the Chief Executive of the borough, as he closed the meeting which approved progress to the next stage. The metaphorical use of Arctic explorer's language seemed apt enough to the working group: their task had turned out to be much more a plunge into the unknown than they had ever imagined it would be.

It was clear that the project would never succeed without the right people to run it. The hands-on project leaders needed extraordinary qualities. Motivating those who have lived for a long time in a state of demotivation calls for particular skills. Keeping such people motivated after the initial novelty of a new project has worn off is even harder.

Such a person requires the charisma to become a role model, but also needs to be sufficiently similar to the volunteers for them to be able to identify with him or her. There is chemistry involved here, and in considering the scenario, we must accept that this is not the stuff of which ordinary project managers are made. Many of the problems, though, are of a similar type, cast into sharp relief by the harsh light of the difficult circumstances and harsh demands of real life.

To complicate things further, it was clear that more than one such individual was going to be required, in order to carry forward both aspects of the project with reasonable speed. The people appointed therefore needed to be team players, amongst their other qualities.

The working group turned for help to the personnel department of the council, but this was no use. The situation was too different from the mainstream for the selection procedures to be transferable. Too few definable benchmarks were available, and some of the standard modes of comparison were incapable of giving weight to the truly important aspects of the case.

Once again, it was Peter Hackforth's advice that came to be followed. He said that the project organization should be configured around the combination of skills available, rather than the other way round. 'All these blokes are drop-outs', he said, referring to the project leaders available. 'That's why they are attracted to the job. It's no use expecting them to slot into a job description, and deal with others according to an organizational model. They will lead organically, but they will not manage according to a prescription, at least not very reliably.'

It was therefore decided to integrate the project vertically, as two teams, each with a project leader, who would guide them through the complete process of training and construction.

Horizontal integration, and tiers of management, would be avoided in all aspects of the project. There would be a council of management. This would be a round-table organization, composed of the working group, the two project leaders, and a construction manager, who might also be the chief designer. The council would delegate tasks via one or more of its members, and empower them to employ, for instance, specialist contractors or design consultants direct.

One sticking point was that this arrangement completely defied all the local authority public accountability policies for testing the market and demonstrating that value had been obtained. As there were already a number of councillors who had been heard to mutter that too much was being invested in a highly risky, hare-brained scheme, which could have been spent with solid benefit on housing, it became a difficult matter politically.

The support of the Chief Executive was crucial at this time. Nevertheless, the issue could have forced reorganization along more conventional, but less practical, lines, had not a cigarette company, Kelso Tobacco, which had a factory in the borough, come forward as a sponsor. There were ethical objections to this too, but it was agreed in the end that help from a local employer was something not to be turned away.

THE PARTIES INVOLVED

The working group defined the stakeholders of the project as follows:

- project sponsors: local authority, Kelso Tobacco
- local homeless
- volunteers
- designers
- local authority planners, etc.
- Employment Agency
- specialist contractors and tradesmen
- neighbours
- Department of Health and Social Security

- Department of Employment
- families
- other homeless people.

FINANCIAL STRUCTURE, AND ITS IMPLICATIONS

Kelso Tobacco had agreed to participate in the project by providing the services of a purchasing manager, and funding the purchase of all hardware and building materials within an agreed budget. They would also have a seat on the council of management.

This left the local authority with the following:

- providing the site
- salaries of all employed staff
- insurance
- telephone and other communication costs
- fees to professional advisors
- contracts with specialist contractors
- payments to all statutory bodies
- payments to trainees
- any overspend of the budget.

The local authority was also committed to completing and operating the day centre for a period of 5 years at least, and to naming it 'The Kelso Day Centre'. 'So we get all the risk, but only some of the glory', commented the Chief Executive wryly.

Responsibility for cost and certification of payments lay with the council of management. As this was a local-authority body, this transferred ultimate responsibility back to the council, although of course external employed members might be liable to the council in contract or in tort if they failed in their duties.

DEFINING THE DESIGNERS AND THEIR BRIEF

The decisions to date had mostly led the project away from conventional patterns.

Now there was the need to select suitable designers and brief them, and it became clear that the constraints on the design were about buildability more than anything else. Of course, there was also the inescapable need for fitness for purpose, *commodity, firmness and delight*, and the need to meet planning standards as in any other project. Some of those involved thought that the design ought to express the unusual aspects of the project in an inventive way. A university suggested that the design be made the subject of a student competition, and in fact proceeded to do this. A well-known architect who had been born in Stratney did a perspective sketch of his suggested scheme unasked, and had it published in an architectural weekly.

None of these designs satisfied the council, although a number had strong points to recommend them. Some tried too hard to be interesting, at a cost in either buildability or usability, whilst others were boring in the way that simple, low-cost, timber-framed, single-storey buildings can be. A breakthrough came when a local teacher, who had been involved in studies of the remains of a Roman villa excavated in the borough, got her class of 11-year-olds to do an imaginative sketch of the new day centre as a courtyard scheme on the Roman model.

This won general approval from the points of view of benefits in use, where the protected central space was thought a very good feature, and of construction, in which good use of the existing party walls of the plot could be made. The brief was therefore redefined in these terms, and made the subject of a limited competition to a list developed from those who had shown interest, and those whom the director of planning suggested, plus one or two suggestions which came from the working group themselves. By this point, the search was really for an aesthetic and functional solution, the building form and construction being generally defined.

Key issues: exercise

The project has gone pretty well so far, all things considered. The project team has been compiled on a considered basis, and the stakeholders are mostly onside; even the sceptics have abated their opposition.

How confident would you be about the project continuing in a successful way? How would you, as chairman of the working group, plan for expected difficulties, particularly where local-authority procedures and the anti-organizational mindset which seems to pervade the pool of available team leaders are concerned? How can a sense of ownership of the project be encouraged amongst its participants? Can the project have a culture of its own? How and when should this be engendered?

Part 3

14

Conclusion

It is in everyone's best interest that effective and efficient teamworking is realized for a construction project. The growth in project management, even for building projects of quite a small size, means that a discipline now exists, the prime concern of which is to enable the construction project team to work together to realize common objectives with the client. Not only will improved teamworking mean the client's time, cost and quality requirements are more likely to be met, but also the consultant and contractor firms that take part are more likely to realize their expected profits for having taken part.

Teams, whether as choirs or for construction projects, have a great number of things in common. They comprise very different people, each with very diverse skills and knowledge which when combined allow them to achieve that which they could never do on their own. Of utmost importance to the success of *any* team in any field is the 'spirit' or 'ethos' it embodies and to which all its members subscribe. 'Team spirit' essentially entails the belief of everyone who belongs to the team in the capability of the team to be successful in what it undertakes. It also means the personal belief of each team member in the others and what they can do. It conversely means that all team members must be able to demonstrate their capabilities to the others. Confidence in and commitment to the other team members has to be foundation for any successful team. 'Working for each other' is much more than just a catchphrase.

It is self-evident is that the creation of 'team spirit' takes time as people get to know each other and their strengths and weaknesses and to trust each other. This is in the nature of human beings. 'Team spirit' is also reinforced by success, which itself takes time in order for the team to carry out whatever task it is required to undertake. In fact, the need to develop over time through familiarity and achievement has been the incentive to promote longer-term 'partnership' arrangements between clients, consultants and contractors for construction project teams. However, most construction projects are still likely to be wanted by clients for whom long-term and continuous partnerships with consultant and contractors are not practical. They may only have a need for a project very occasionally, perhaps because of the nature of their own business. Also, changing financial circumstances related to their own particular businesses' 'marketplace' may mean that planned projects have to be 'shelved' unexpectedly. So this makes it impractical or impossible, and probably even unfair, for a client to make promises of guaranteed future work to any consultant or contractor 'partner' in the long term. The safest assumption to make about the creation and sustaining of a construction project team is that it can only really be practically considered on a project by project basis. What is therefore vitally important is that each particular project develops and sustains as much 'partnering' atmosphere that generates positive cooperation between team members as is reasonably possible just for its duration. Apart from a fair and expected direct monetary 'reward' for taking part in the project itself, the other indirect 'reward' for any good team player can obviously be the enhancement of his or her firm's reputation and recommendation of that firm by the client and any other participating consultant or contractor.

For this 'team spirit' to flourish on any 'one-off' project, this book recommends in its preceding chapters that participating firms – and especially project managers, whether in house to the client or externally appointed – should apply all the following six 'understandings' to the joining, formation and management of the construction project team. Gaining these understandings and applying the lessons of their implications *in total* should also ensure that 'teamworking' is not only pleasurable for all the individual people who take part but also profitable for the participating firms to which they belong.

UNDERSTANDING 1

That a construction project is *generic* in terms of *particular* processes, people and products involved but that it is *unique* in the *specific* combination of client, location, time, social/economic/political environment and supplier firms that take part.

The implications of this can be seen in the issues raised in the Argent House, Berzozil and self-build for the homeless case studies.

UNDERSTANDING 2

That a construction project combines the efforts and interests of different *business firms*, each responsible for the cost aspect of a major part of the whole project. This differentiates them from 'projects' carried out within a single business firm. Each firm's own *business* interests will be affected for good or ill not only by the *performance* of itself but also by the *performance* of all the other participating firms whose *efforts* directly affect its own.

The implications of this can be seen in the issues raised in the Berzozil and self-build for the homeless case studies.

UNDERSTANDING 3

A construction project requires the establishment of a *temporary* organization both within and between the different participating firms. There are both benefits and disadvantages due to the temporary nature of the 'organization'. The benefits are that the right culture and arrangement can be instantly created to match the particular purpose of the project — the disadvantage is that there is only a short time in which the right culture and arrangement can be created. There is also the fact that a number of participating firms — the specialist contractors who construct the later elements — may join an 'organization' that has already been established in their absence.

The implications of this can be seen in the issues raised in the Berzozil and self-build for the homeless case studies.

UNDERSTANDING 4

That construction projects on the human level comprise people who are all very different in terms of 'personality' and 'temperament' and have 'natural' roles that they would best play in any team. Each individual also has his or her own 'thinking' style, and whether teams work or not so often depends on both the right combination of these different styles and the acceptance of each person's acceptances of the other's differences. However, it has to be accepted that construction project teams are formed with people who come from the appointed firms — the appointment of which is based on their ability to deliver a 'product' or 'service' to the right standard for the right price and on time. No guarantees can be given that any team will automatically have the best people combination. Even at appointment stage, when a client might wish for a particular person from a particular firm to be the one involved in the project, other circumstances within the firm might not always make that possible.

The implications of this can be seen in the issues raised in the Argent House and Berzozil case studies.

UNDERSTANDING 5

That a construction project team comprises a range of different disciplines and stakeholders, all of whom have diverse interests in the project based on their professional and other backgrounds. Essentially, the main 'team' can be considered as the prime design and construction disciplines, each of which represents a particular 'tradition' of views and approaches towards a construction project. Included in that main team is the client, whose 'tradition' can range across the whole spectrum of professional, commercial or industrial backgrounds found in society. The wider team can considered as all others who one way or another have a stake in the project, with such wide-ranging interests as funding and being an adjacent owner. Even the particular design and construction disciplines may have their specific interests within their overall discipline (for example an *architect* whose interest is in a *classical* design style).

The implications of this can be seen in the issues raised in the Ark case study.

UNDERSTANDING 6

That a construction project team works with information in that they exchange it between each other and should add value to it at each pass from one to the other. The information with which they work has a paper-based tradition of being in the form of briefs, drawings, specifications, schedules, bills and programmes, supplemented by instructions, orders, invoices and receipts to show that each participant's 'work' has been completed, used and verified. However, what this information actually represents is each project team member's 'knowledge' being applied to realizing the aims of the project through the processes of briefing, design, cost control and construction resource management – all of which more often that not come about as a result of individual or group decision-making. Which itself can only be sensibly based on relevant, accurate and complete information being available in an understandable form at the right time to those team members who need to make a decision. Emerging information technologies allow advantages for effective and efficient information exchange that were not possible with paper-based methods. Instantaneous shared information, such as a computer image of the proposed building, allows instantaneous shared 'knowledge' as each team member can contribute, allowing interactive decision-making agreed as being the best option by all the team. Best of all, clients can understand what is being proposed if those images are 3D and possibly animated, better than they can with any paper-based 2D drawing, with backing data on such things as cost and performance so that they can be assured that their requirements are being met as they are proposed.

The implications of this can be seen in the issues raised in the Argent House case study.

Working in teams is instinctive to human nature. The need for others (Handy, 1997) is fundamental to any individual for knowing who they are and where they fit into the broader scheme of things. 'Teamwork is individuals working together to accomplish more than they could alone, but, more than that it can be exciting, satisfying and enjoyable' (Woodcock, 1985). The more committed the members of the team are to each other, given they have the appropriate skills and knowledge, the greater the achievement in terms of a quality outcome whatever field of endeavour they apply themselves to. Examples abound of this both currently and throughout history. Inspired leadership that displays a passionate belief in the aims of any group's activity is about the surest way of imbibing a 'team spirit'. It is catching! However, unless that group as a whole understands its own nature, aims and objectives; comprises the right disciplines; is attractive to individuals' own interests to get their commitment; has individual members who accept each other as different; is organized to ensure the right resources, responsibilities and relationships that are needed to get work done are in place; and shares knowledge through efficient and effective information exchange, 'team spirit' will be quickly dissipated if ever it is created. If, as is the case with a construction project team, the 'group' is also a group of businesses, then it is also vital that they make a profit and enhance their reputation and business from the venture. They certainly do not want the opposite to happen!

Construction project teams work intuitively and naturally and have the benefit of knowing exactly who the ultimate 'customer' is for their efforts, in the shape of the commissioning client. As individuals they also always have very clear specialized roles to play and basic skills and experience to fulfil them — from designer to tradesman. As particular people, they have developed personal abilities to compromise — because they will always have to as project solutions always require some sort of compromise between different interests. These are their strengths. Their weaknesses are in those areas covered by this book and it is those that cause the industry's participating firms to be less profitable than they could be. A lack of any of the 'understandings' of these areas and their application will create a weakness in any construction project team. The price paid will be loss of profit or reputation by some team-member firm.

Eliminating these weaknesses and building on the construction project team's natural strengths in the ways suggested in this book will make them work profitably.

Appendices

Appendix 1: Personal styles

The following descriptions are from standard industry tests concerning the most natural roles that people are likely to play in teams and about individuals' personal temperament preference type. The first comes from Belbin's work, which studied teams in industry organizations over many years (Belbin, 1997), and the second is the from Keirsey temperament sorter from the work of Myers–Briggs (Briggs Myers, 1988).

Both are self-assessment tests in which the individuals answer questions about themselves and how they tend to react to various events and happenings in their life as well as how they feel about a variety of things. The way the tests are framed as questions and interpreted are such that no one get a particular outcome that is not a true reflection of how he or she has answered the questions. Results are usually accepted by those who take the tests as being a fairly true reflection of themselves and how they are as a person at that particular time. It is a fact that taking tests some years apart may show changes, and this is to be expected as people do 'change' as they mature and experience life through both their work and their social life experience. However, how people are as personality types and the way they operate in relation to others are fairly fixed and make for the difference between people.

The outcomes of both these tests show people that they have strengths and weaknesses as individuals and in their relationship with others. It is also true that 'opposites' — which are revealed by the Keirsey temperament sorter — can work well together and 'similars' may clash on a personal level. Similarly, people who have the same sort of *natural* team role style might clash and a balance of different ones may work much better in a team context. What is very obvious about construction project teams is that they are very much appointed because of their different discipline skills and experience and *not* on the basis of their different personal styles. A construction project by its very definition is not likely to have a balanced team in terms of personality types and styles by design — only by default. For example it would be very difficult for a client, or the project manager, to insist on a particular person from an appointed firm because of their *personality* rather than their *availability*, *skill*, or *experiential knowledge*! It is also questionable whether in any but very large and prestigious projects any such tests could be justifiably requested — even then it is most likely that the criterion for selecting and appointing any individual key person is more likely to be his or her *experience* rather than *personality*. By virtue of their very work, most people in the construction industry find ways of getting on with each other — one way or another — because they have to in order to complete their own work and in order to eventually be financially rewarded for doing so.

Therefore the following tables of people types, strengths, weaknesses, relationships and roles are useful in understanding how other people are likely to be — and what their 'behaviour' is exhibiting about themselves. It also therefore gives other team members who have to work with others, and especially project managers and leaders, 'clues' as to how people and their relationships are best handled given the roles they have to fulfil. Even if these tests are not formally taken, knowing the strengths and weaknesses of different role and preference types is useful for management. The project manager and leaders need to ensure that those roles and preference styles that are *not* naturally occurring in the appointed team are drawn out from the existing team members or deliberately brought in from outside.

Combining the ideas about how people are and how they perform in teams can give the project manager or particular team leader an idea of what may be lacking or even going wrong in the team on a personal level — and what can be done about it.

BELBIN TEST

This shows *natural* team roles that people can play, their strengths, and allowable and *not* allowable weaknesses for good teamworking. Answering a seven-section questionnaire with ten questions to which the person allocates ten points to answers becomes interpreted as

Table A1.1. Natural team roles indicated by the Belbin test (Belbin, 1997)

Team role contribution	Characteristics	Allowable weaknesses	Non-allowable weaknesses
Plant	Creative, imaginative, unorthodox. Solves difficult problems	Ignores details. Too preoccupied to communicate effectively	Strong ownership of idea when cooperation with others would yield better results
Resource investigator	Extrovert, enthusiastic, communicative. Explores opportunities. Develops contacts	Overoptimistic. Loses interest once initial enthusiasm has passed	Letting clients down by neglecting the follow-up arrangements
Coordinator	Mature, confident, a good chairperson. Clarifies goals, promotes decision-making, delegates well	Can be seen as manipulative. Delegates personal work	Taking credit for the effort of the team
Shaper	Challenging, dynamic, thrives on pressure. Has the drive and courage to overcome obstacles	Can provoke others. Hurts people's feelings	Inability to recover situation with good humour or apology
Monitor evaluator	Sober, strategic and discerning. Sees all options. Judges accurately	Lacks drive and ability to inspire others. Overly critical	Cynicism without logic
Teamworker	Cooperative, mild, perceptive and diplomatic. Listens, builds, averts friction, calms the waters	Indecisive in a crunch situation. Can be easily influenced.	Avoiding situations that may entail pressure
Implementer	Disciplined, reliable, conservative and efficient. Turns ideas into practical actions	Somewhat inflexible. Slow to respond to new possibilities.	Obstructing change
Completer	Painstaking, conscientious, anxious. Searches out errors and omissions. Delivers on time	Inclined to worry unduly. Reluctant to delegate. Can be a 'nit-picker'	Obsessive behaviour

Table A1.1. Cont.

Specialist	Single-minded, self-starting, dedicated. Provides knowledge and skills in rare supply	Contributes on only a narrow front. Dwells on technicalities. Overlooks the 'big picture'	Ignoring factors outside own area of competence

showing the roles that person *most naturally* fulfils, those that can be *managed* and those that should be avoided (Table A1.1).

It should be emphasized that this test gives a broad picture of any individual which is generally true at the time, and by their own efforts individuals can change over time through experience — especially in reducing their weaknesses.

MYERS-BRIGGS TYPE INDICATOR — KEIRSEY TEMPERAMENT SORTER

This shows four different *opposite* temperament types, of which any individual can be a particular combination, and the relationship factors that are likely to exist between the opposites. After answering a set of 70 questions of opposite tendencies, the interpretation of the answers shows an individual that he or she is a particular combination of the factors shown in Table A1.2 — of which there can be 16 combinations.

People will generally have a *preference* on these scales although sometimes they come out 50%–50% so for example they may be balanced between introvert and extrovert. So any individual can come out as an extrovert–sensing–feeling–perception type, an introvert–intuition–thinking–judgement type, etc. However, what is most useful knowing these preferences in yourself and other people is how they can affect relationships. A précis of this is given in Table A1.3.

One of the useful things is to have a balance in a team of these personal preferences when it comes to 'problem solving' so that a process of *sensing* (getting the facts), *intuition* (considering the possibilities), *thinking* (considering consequences) and *feeling* (understanding the impact) can be gone through to come to the best considered solution.

Again, this test will show people's *preferences* at a given time, and the outcome is usually generally true by their own self-recognition.

Table A1.2. Temperament types in the Myers–Briggs type indicator

Extroversion–introversion	*Sensing–intuition*
How we prefer to give/receive energy of focus our attention	How we prefer to gather information
Thinking–feeling	*Judgement–perception*
How we prefer to make decisions	How we prefer to handle the outside world

Table A1.3. Preferences in the Myers–Briggs scale and how they can affect relationships

Extroverts	*Introverts*
Prefer action and outer world	Prefer ideas and the inner world
Should recognize that Introverts need space but encouragement and you need their depths to learn from	*Should recognize that Extroverts need activity and people and you need their inspiration*
Sensing–thinking types	*Sensing–feeling types*
Are interested in facts and analysis and apply their feelings impersonally	Although interested in facts, relate their analysis to themselves and others
Remember that Intuitives have wonderful ideas and vision and don't expect detailed applications	*Remember that Thinkers can appear cold and impersonal but you need to develop your thinking*
Intuitive–thinking types	*Intuitive–feeling types*
Preferences results in an interest in possibilities and have theoretical, technical or executive abilities	Combinations, although interested in possibilities, prefer tackling new projects and unsolved problems
Remember that Sensers need your vision but you need their attention to detail	*Remember Feelers need harmony and affirmation and need more time to talk things out*
Judging types	*Perceivers*
Are decisive and like planning and control	Are flexible, live spontaneously, and understand and adapt readily
Be aware that Perceivers love change and spontaneity and can bring things to life that you cannot	*Remember that your adaptability can drive Judgers mad but that their decisions are final*

However, as people continue to understand themselves they may change preferences of their own accord – especially if it helps them overcome their own perceived weaknesses (Oakland and Morris, 1997).

These tests are readily available from management-training sources and often used on project management training courses such as the one described in Appendix 2. They could be actually given to team members on projects – preferably by consensus rather that coercion.

Getting individuals to do them should not be that difficult, as it is interesting for the individuals concerned as helping them to know themselves better and how to improve their relationships with others with whom they have to work. More often than not people see this as a 'fun' thing to do and do not see it as a threat to reveal them for negative reasons.

Appendix 2: Training programme

The following is an outline description of a training programme for construction project management designed for busy practitioners.* Although the intention of the course is to prepare candidates for taking an Association of Project Managers examination it also lays a great stress on the necessity for *teamworking* for the successful management of projects.

The course has been designed and developed by the authors by combining the experience of many years of applied academic research into construction management with a view from practice of the need for project management skills. The need for project management for building has grown over the last 15 years in the UK with most clients – both private and public – requiring a 'project manager' as well as all the traditional disciplines of the building team. Architects, engineers, quantity surveyors and builders are all wishing to be recognized as 'project managers' by acquiring those additional skills needed on top of their own traditional design, cost and construction skills and knowledge. This course is very practical and uses the candidate's own 'project' experience as the basis of a learning approach. By combining days at the university with work at home and assessing a major assignment, it helps traditional disciplines to start to think 'project' rather than thinking just about 'architectural or engineering design' or 'cost' or 'construction'. Candidates have to apply project management

---

* Taken from the prospectus for the Short Course in Construction Project Management, Department of Construction Management and Engineering, The University of Reading, in conjunction with Johnston & Mather, 1999.

201

principles to a series of case studies — both at the university and during homeworking — in order to keep seeing the broader picture required by a project manager. Both the teaching and the case study working bring out the teamworking skills as being a key to success in applying new project management skills and knowledge to a series of simulated building projects. The course curriculum is as follows.

Course Philosophy

AIM

The aim of the Course is to provide experienced construction professionals with the additional skills and knowledge that will enable them to practice as recognised project managers on behalf of their clients. It is accepted that architects, engineers, surveyors and builders have certain project management skills and knowledge acquired through the experience of their existing professional practice. Therefore the approach to learning is to put didactic teaching into practical *project* contexts with which candidates are already familiar, but in a way that always brings out the *project management* view in contrast to the *design, cost and construction* views which the candidates to the course bring from their backgrounds.

Although the Course is suitable for *all* construction professionals it is particularly aimed at those who are *designers* — that is to say architects and engineers who want to add a recognised project management service dimension to their business. Its detailed content also caters for the small practice and emphasises the *business* aspect for project management — both for the practitioner as well as their client.

BASIS OF CURRICULUM

The Course's curriculum is based upon nationally recognised subject frameworks of the skills and knowledge needed to be a client's project manager. They are:

- The Association for Project Management (APM) Body of Knowledge. This is a similar framework against which courses for project management can be accredited for covering the knowledge and skills needed by a project manager belonging to this Association. The Association also sets its own examination for project managers wishing to be members. It is the UK body affiliated to the International Association of Project Managers.

- The Course also uses its University base to draw upon the internationally recognised research excellence in *construction project management* of the Department of Construction Management & Engineering. Published reports into various *project management* subject areas — accepted and used by the industry at large — form a core part of its learning base.

The Course's programme recognises the fact that candidates are busy practitioners who can ill afford to spend very much time away from their day-to-day professional practice. It also seeks to give candidates the opportunity to make their acquired training count for as much as possible in leading to wider recognised qualifications beyond the awarding of the Certificate of Attendance. The following time and place pattern recognises this.

Part 1

These two days, in residence at the University, are used to cover the team-building aspects of Project Management, and introduce modes of effective communication, using IT.

Part 2

This interactive exercise is carried out in teams via electronic media including the Course's dedicated web page on the Internet. It brings together the learning outcomes of Part 1, and places emphasis both on the logical imperative in dealing with complexity, and on the fundamental importance of successful relationships with stakeholders.

Distance Learning Workbooks

These two paper-based workbooks (100 pages each) cover the aspects of Project Management in detail, and reinforce learning with exercises and activity reports.

Part 3

This second pair of days in residence at the University covers financial, legal and other statutory elements, and builds upon previous exercise work to circumscribe the whole of the APMP syllabus. A computer practical is included.

Part 4: Assessed Assignment

This exercise, undertaken individually from the workplace, results in a comprehensive report of about 3000 words, which is the assessed outcome of the course.

Timetable

Part 1
Friday 1 9.00 am
Personal introductions and Introduction to the Course

SESSION 1: PROJECT MANAGEMENT & TEAMWORKING
Teamwork exercise
Lecture: Understanding Project Management and Sharing Common
Objectives
Discussion: The Project Manager's Role

Break
Lecture: Organisations & Change
Discussion: Delighting the Client
Review & Discussion: The Essence of Project Management

Lunch
Exercise: Negotiation
Lecture: The Financing of Projects

Break
Lecture: Risk Management
Exercise: Negotiation 2

Dinner
Exercise: Project Inception – Convincing your Client that your Team will
work.

Saturday
SESSION 2: IMPROVING THE PROJECT PROCESS
Project Briefing
Exercise: Brief Definition
Lecture: Value Management

Break
Lecture: Quality and Projects
Exercise: Team Strategy in Developing the Brief

Lunch
Lecture: Alternative Forms of Procurement

SESSION 3: PM QUALIFICATION
Lecture: The Route to Qualification
Exercise: Decision Making for the Client

Break
Introduction to Part 2.
Exercise: Case Study
Group assignment Briefing, Intro to BS
Plenary Session & Review
CLOSE 6 pm

Part 3
Friday 9.00 am
SESSION 4: INFORMATION MANAGEMENT
Group Presentation, Feedback & Review: Berzozil Railway Project

Coffee on the run
Lecture: Cost Estimating & Control

Lunch
Lecture: Design Management
Exercise: Managing Design & Procurement

Break
Lecture: Business/Marketing for PM
Introduction: IE2 Project

Break
Exercise: Putting It Together

Dinner
Lecture: The Leadership and Motivation of People

Saturday 8.30 am
Lecture: Use of IT to Improve the Project Process
IT for Project Management
(Practical in Computer Lab)

Break
Workshop: Project Lifecycle
Start up And Close out

Break
Exercise: Project Lifecycle

Lunch
SESSION 5: THE LEGISLATIVE FRAMEWORK
Lecture: the Legal Context
Exercise: Defining the Legal Position

Break
Lecture: Safety & Industrial Relations
Workshop: CDM & Quality Management

Break
Plenary Session & Review
CLOSE 6 pm

Course Curriculum

(By Teaching at the University and Candidates Own Study and Workbooks
at home with IT support as required)

   The Course Curriculum has been developed over the last year through
discussions with professional bodies and pilot courses with practitioners.
It is concerned as much with the method of delivery as the subjects themselves and draws upon the candidate's existing knowledge through

interactive teaching and by learning in workshops and exercises with feedback discussion. The subjects covered through Lecture teaching, Seminar workshops, Recommended reading, Workbook guidance and candidates homeworking study are as follows:

Design Management

The aim of this subject is to teach the means by which the project manager can manage the design process of the consultants and specialist trade contractors. Topics include:

- *Designer Selection and Management*
- *Design Control, Review and Change*
- *Design Management Systems: BS 7000 Part 4.*

Quality Management

The aim of this subject is to teach the means by which the project manager can manage project quality. Topics include:

- *Delighting Clients*
- *The ISO 9000 Standard/TQM*
- *The Project Control Plan*

Cost Control

The aim of this subject is to teach the means by which the project manager can manage the cost of the project from inception to completion. Topics include:

- *Cost Planning Stages*
- *Cost Data Sources*
- *Cost Scheduling and Control*

Value Management

The aim of this subject is to teach the means by which the project manager can support the client and other team members in judging value in project decision-making. Topics include:

- *Value Hierarchy*
- *Function Analysis System Techniques (Fast)*
- *Value Management Workshops*

Information Technology

The aim of this subject is to teach the means by which the project manager can best utilise emerging IT tools for communication between project team members. Topics include:

- *Design and Construction Integrating Systems*
- *Project Management Systems*
- *Internet-based Tools for Project Management*

Methods of Procurement

The aim of this subject is to teach the means by which the project manager can assess the most appropriate form of design and construction procurement for the project. Topics include:

- *Risks, Roles and Relationships*
- *Best Practice of Trad., CM, and D&B*
- *Partnership Approaches*

Teamworking

The aim of this subject is to teach the means by which the project manager can understand how people work in teams and how they can be best managed. Topics include:

- *Self-analysis of People for Team Roles*
- *Human Basis of Good Teamwork*
- *Nature of Construction Project Teams*

Business/Marketing

The aim of this subject is to teach the means by which the project manager can understand the fundamental principles of business and marketing. Topics include:

- *Reasons and Methods for Marketing*
- *Business Plan and Marketing Action Plan*
- *Product, Placement, Pricing and Promotion*

Project Management

The aim of this subject is to teach the means by which the project manager can understand the fundamental principles of *project management*. Topics include:

- *Definitions of project, project manager and project management*
- *Different types of project and difference between projects and operations*
- *Role of Project Manager, Client and Team*
- *The overall process, BS 6079 and DIS 10006*

Organisation Design

The aim of this subject is to teach the means by which the project manager can understand how the design of the project organisation is related to the company organisations of all the participating firms. Topics include:

- *Project organisation*
- *Company organisations*

Leadership

The aim of this subject is to teach the means by which the project manager can lead the people in the project team and the client. Topics include:

- *Leadership as a form of personal power*
- *Motivation without using management authority*
- *Delegation, responsibility and making best use of resources in time*

Negotiation

The aim of this subject is to teach the means by which the project manager can get agreement with people throughout the life of the project. Topics include:

- *Gaining agreement through 'win–win' approaches*
- *Defusing dangerous situations and resolving conflict*

Risk Management

The aim of this subject is to teach the means by which the project manager can understand how to manage project risk on behalf of the client. Topics include:

- *Identification and assessment of hazards and risks*
- *Hazard and risk avoidance, control and mitigation*
- *Documentary tools for controlling the processes*

Project Financing and Appraisal

The aim of this subject is to teach the means by which the project manager can understand how funds can be raised for the project. Topics include:

- *Types of financial structure and their consequence*
- *Sources of funding*
- *The expectations of funding bodies*
- *Investment appraisals and benefit analysis*

Project Environment and Strategy

The aim of this subject is to teach the means by which the project manager can understand the project in relationship to its physical, organisational and socio-economic environment. Topics include:

- *External influences and their impact*
- *Seeing the 'big picture', vision and scope*
- *Team role in developing strategy*
- *The problems of managing multiple project programmes*

Project Lifecycle, Commissioning and Close-out

The aim of this subject is to teach the means by which the project manager can understand the important issues involved with the project lifecycle. Topics include:

- *Allowing for future change*
- *Costs viewed over the lifecycle of a building*
- *Progression of project phases*
- *Managing changing requirements*
- *Document audit trails and contractual matters*
- *Commissioning and handover to client*

Legal Context

The aim of this subject is to teach the means by which the project manager can develop a broad understanding of the legal issues involved in a project. Topics include:

- *Common and Statute Law*
- *The laws of contract and tort*
- *The responsibility and liability of the project manager*
- *The relationship between UK law and EU directives*

Safety and Industrial Relations

The aim of this subject is to teach the means by which the project manager can understand the nature of health and safety and industrial relation laws. Topics include:

- *Health and Safety Legislation and the responsibility of parties*
- *The CDM Regulations, and their general approach and requirements*
- *Enforcement of the legal requirements*
- *Overview of employment law*

Communication, Co-ordination and Control

The aim of this subject is to teach the means by which the project manager can understand how to ensure all parties communicate, co-ordinate their efforts and the overall process is controlled. Topics include:

- *Setting up effective communication systems to suit project culture*
- *Measuring performance against targets*
- *Success/failure criteria*
- *Expediting through cost and schedule control*

Mobilisation, Work Definition, Planning and Scheduling

The aim of this subject is to teach the means by which the project manager can analyse through breakdown structures various categories of product, work, cost and organisation in order to focus on aspects of the project. Topics include:

- *Initiation and identification of physical and human resources*
- *Breakdown structures and plans*
- *Networks, Gantt Charts and Critical Path Analysis*

Management of Change

The aim of this subject is to teach the means by which the project manager can understand the relationship of organisations and systems to change. Topics include:

- *Change control*
- *Processes and their effect on formal undertakings*
- *The consequences of lack of control*

The aim of the following simulated live projects and workbook is to let candidates apply the lessons from the above subject areas in teams for good project management practice.

Projects used for Learning

The following simulated projects are used in workshop exercises by the candidates, working in teams at the University and in teams and as individuals at home:

Project 1: Project Inception: a Central London Site

Description of Candidates' Work
The candidates firstly work to identify the wishes and needs of their client, and establish a brief. In doing this they consider the project environment (one constrained by space and the proximity of a railway and a flyover) and identify stakeholders, and analyse their needs. They then consider forms of procurement, and present a strategy for the initial phases of the project.

Learning Outcome

To develop an understanding of how the nature of the requirements and the constraints of a site have a formative effect on a project.

Project 2: Negotiation: Building a Village School

Description of Candidates' Work

The scenario is one of difficult timescale and disruptive local influences in an externally-funded building project in Africa. The task is to identify win–win situations that turn these situations into opportunities for progress.

Learning Outcome

To learn to distinguish between important and unimportant factors in working with a tight timescale.

To develop a greater understanding of the opportunities for recognizing the needs of others and obtaining their support.

Project 3: Commercial Redevelopment of Railway Land in Eastern Europe

Description of Candidates' Work

The candidates work in teams during their time away from the University (Module 2). They communicate from their individual workplaces, making use of electronic tools. They present their conclusions and rationale to the whole group during Module 3. Their tasks consist of the following, in which they are expected to demonstrate their understanding of project management systems and tools:

- Analyse the present situation.
- The implications for the Railway in adopting a customer-centred approach.
- Advise on the possible strategies for redeveloping the railway station and land, taking into account the likely effects on the railway operation.
- Report on the feasibility of the commercial redevelopment, including the options available for finance, and the likely position of stakeholders.
- A report on the project management resources likely to be required to progress the matter.

Learning Outcome

- To test the techniques learned to date in a scenario of adequate scope to bring the various aspects together and demonstrate the conflicts that can occur within a project.
- To make testing analysis one of the aspects of the assignment.
- To make a presentation emphasising the need to cope with complexity and develop one matter in the context of others.

Project 4: Restoration and Conversion of the Old Town Hall, Warminster, Wiltshire

(Project used as an individual homework exercise by the candidates, the outcome of which is used in part for their assessment.)

Description of Candidates' Work
The candidates work in a realistic scenario that unfolds in time, as stakeholders from planning officers to local pressure groups have their say. The client's brief results from muddled thinking on his part, and adjustments are needed if the project is to be viable.

Learning Outcome
The candidates demonstrate flexibility and an ability to respond to a changing scene. They demonstrate a wide variety of skills, including analysing a difficult situation, developing a brief and strategy, identifying the resources required, and programming the procurement process.

Assessment
Candidates are assessed through a 3000 word Assignment based on their working on Module 4. Criteria for passing the Assignment and receiving the Certificate will be:

• To demonstrate a clear understanding of the subjects listed in the APMP syllabus, to the levels indicated, within the context of the case study.
• To show competence in the employment of this knowledge.

Workbook used for Practice Application

The Henley Distance Learning Workbook 'Making Projects Happen' is issued and used by candidates in the *Homeworking* Parts 2 and 4 of the Course and —

• acts as a revision for teaching and over-learning on all the subject areas taught in Parts 1 and 3 at the University through the workbook's text.
• provides further live project application examples of project management practice through the workbook's audio and video tapes
• provides exercises in applying project management principles to their own practice through workbook's worksheets

The Workbook also gives the candidate a wider view about the application of project management principles than just to construction projects. It also shows them how their own organisation's *corporate* management relates to *project* management. The application worksheets cover the following topic areas:

- *Projects and the corporate plan*
- *Involved parties*
- *Key project parameters*
- *Project definition report*
- *Milestone planning*
- *Work package scope planning*
- *Responsibility charts*
- *Risk monitoring*
- *Risk correction*
- *Risk assessment*
- *Configuration management*

It would also be expected that the outcomes of these lesson applications would also be demonstrated in their assessed Assignment that comprises Part 5.

Assessment and Affiliations

Assessment

- Candidates are assessed through a 3000 word Assignment based on their working on Project 4
- Criteria for passing the assignment and receiving their Certificate will be as shown for *Project No. 4 in Projects used for Learning* section

Affiliations

- The Course is a Short Course from the Department of Construction Management & Engineering which is part of the Faculty of Urban and Regional Studies. The Department received a 5A* rating in the recent Research Selectivity Round, which is the highest, and the Department is internationally recognised as a centre of excellence for construction project management. It also runs a full-time MSc Degree in Construction Management and a part-time MSc Degree in Project Management. In its close association with the construction industry it provides specialised Certificated short courses in for example the Construction Management procurement method.

The awarded Certificate would therefore carry weight nationally and internationally in the field of construction project management. With regard to Europe, the Course's development is linked into an EU Leonardo Europroject, the purpose of which is to see how the training and recognition of construction project managers might be harmonised across the Member States.

References

Adair, J. (1983). *Effective Leadership.* Pan, London.

Addis, W. (1994). *The Art of the Structural Engineer.* Artemis, London.

Armstrong, G., Saunders, J., Wong, V. and Kotler, P. (1996). *The Principles of Marketing.* Prentice-Hall, Englewood Cliffs, NJ.

Beard, D. (1995). *Leadership and the Motivation of People.* Lecture, Management Unit, University of Reading, Reading.

Belbin, R. M. (1997). *Team Roles at Work.* Butterworth Heinemann, Oxford.

Bennett, J. and Jayes, S. (1995). *Trusting the Team.* CSSC, University of Reading, Reading.

Bradbury, A. (1997). *NLP for Business Success.* Kogan Page, London.

Briggs Meyers, I. (1988). *Introduction to Type*, 5th edn. Oxford Psychologists Press, Oxford.

British Standards Institution (1997). *Quality Assurance Standards Series.* BSI, Milton Keynes, ISO 9000.

Broadbent, G. (1973). *Design in Architecture.* Wiley, Chichester.

CCPI (1986). *Co-ordinated Construction Project Information Manual.* Co-ordinated Construction Project Information, London.

Chang, R. (1994). *Building a Dynamic Team.* Kogan Page, London.

CIRIA (1997). *Partnering Report.* CIRIA, London.

Cohen, N. (1994). *The Business Plan — Approved.* Gower, Aldershot.

Cornick, T. (1991). *Quality Management for Building Design.* Butterworth, London.

Cornick, T. (1996). *Computer Integrated Building Design.* Chapman and Hall, London.

Cornick, T. and Broomfield, J. (1996). Designing a construction project as a whole business system. *CIB Conference.* Beijing.

215

Cornick, T. *et al.* (1988–1996). SERC research projects and teaching company scheme reports. University of Reading, Reading.

Crosby, P. (1997). *The Absolutes of Leadership.* Jossey-Bas, San Francisco.

CSSC (1991). *Construction Management Forum — Report and Guidance.* Centre for Strategic Studies, University of Reading, Reading.

European Construction Industry Institute (1998). *European Construction Industry Institute News* **2**.

Flanagan, R. and Gray, C. (1989). *The Changing Role of the Specialist Contractor.* Chartered Institute of Building, London.

Frith, J. (1997). *Markets and Marketing.* Lecture notes, Construction Project Management Short Course, University of Reading, Reading.

Goldman, D. (1998). *Working with Emotional Intelligence.* Bantam, London.

Gray, C., Hughes, W. and Bennett, J. (1994). *The Successful Management of Design.* University of Reading, Reading.

Green, S. (1996). A metaphorical analysis of client organisations and the briefing process. *Construction Management and Economics* **14**, 155–164.

Hammer, M. and Champy, J. (1998). *Reengineering the Corporation: A Manifesto for Business Revolution.* HarperCollins, New York.

Handy, C. (1997). *The Hungry Spirit.* Hutchinson Arrow, London.

Harrington, H. J. (1991). *Business Process Improvement.* McGraw-Hill, New York.

HM Treasury Task Force (1997). *Partnership for Prosperity — The Private Finance Initiative.* Public Enquiries Unit, HM Treasury, London.

IAI (1997–1999). Construction Management Domain Committee reports. International Alliance for Interoperability, Business Round Table, London.

Institute of Civil Engineers (1998). *The Engineering and Construction Contract,* 2nd edn. Thomas Telford, London.

JCT (1960 onwards). *Forms of Contract.* Joint Contracts Tribunal, London.

Klean, R. and Ludin, I. (1997). *The People Side of Project Management.* Gower, Aldershot.

Latham, M. (1994). *Constructing the Team.* HMSO, Norwich.

Lawson, B. (1983). *How Designers Think.* Butterworth Architecture, London.

Losoncy, L. E. (1997). *The Motivating Team Leader.* CRC Press, Boca Raton, FL.

Morgan, G. (1986). *Images of Organisations.* Sage, Beverly Hills, CA.

Oakland, J. and Morris, P. (1997). *TQM: A Pictorial Guide for Managers.*

Butterworth Heinemann, Oxford.

Paterson, J. (1980). *Architecture and the Microprocessor.* Wiley, Chichester.

Pearman, H. (1993). *The Ark. Blueprint Extra 10.* Wordsearch, London.

Roberts, J. (1979). *The Unkown Reality*, Vol. 2. Prentice-Hall, Englewood Cliffs, NJ.

Royal Institute of British Architects (1968 onwards). *Plan of Work.* RIBA, London.

Singmaster, D. (1996). Peopling the Ark. *Architect's Journal* **204**, No. 16, 47.

Spinner, M. P. (1997). *Project Management Principles and Practices.* Prentice Hall, Hemel Hempstead.

University of Reading (1997–1999). EU Leonardo da Vince 'Euroconstruction' Project, individual reports. University of Reading, Reading.

Woodcock, M. (1985). *Team Development Manual.* Gower, Aldershot.

Vincent, S. and Wilson Kirkpatrick, S. (1998). *Infoculture.* Thomas Telford, London.

Walton, M. (1989). *The Deming Management Method.* Mercury Books, London.

Young, T. L. (1995). *Leading Projects.* The Industrial Society, London.

Index

agenda
  organization 105
  in temporary organization 107–8,
    112, 113
architect
  benefits of virtual organization to
    124
  design process 75–7
  as designer 35
  role in temporary organization 51
  as supplier members of team 75–7
arrangement
  organization 104
  in temporary organization 107–8,
    112, 113
Association for Project Management
    (APM) Body of Knowledge
    202

Belbin test 195, 196–8
  role types 61, 62, 63
benchmarking 66, 90, 101
business case for forming team
  client's 21–4, 31
  constructor's 26–7, 31
  cost/project manager's 27–8, 31
  designer's 24–5, 31
business objectives 85–102
  benefits and problems of setting
    87–8, 101
  bottom line 86, 101
  method and constraints 88–91,

  101, 102
business plan framework 22–3
business process improvement 88,
    89
business re-engineering 88, 89, 104

client 35
  as customer team member 73–4
  improving effectiveness 14
  role 8
codes of practice 36
computer-aided design (CAD) 76,
    121, 122
construction activities 3
construction management
    procurement process, generic
    phases 6
construction manager
  improving effectiveness 14
  role 9
  whole-building 79–80
construction project team
  basic functional roles 7
  cf. other types of team 4–6
  composition 33, 35
  factors influencing effectiveness
    10–11
  method of working 33, 35–6
  purpose 33, 34–5
  strengths and weaknesses 58–9
construction project teamworking
  first signs of effectiveness 16–17

improving 11–12
improving business of the design/
    construction organization
    12–14
contract administrator, role in
    temporary organization 51
contractor
    as construction manager 35
    main/general 9
contractual systems 36
coordinating construction project
    information (CCPI) 116–17
culture
    definition 64
    diverse 64–5
    organization 104–7
    in temporary organization 107–8,
        112, 113
customer organizations 28

de-escalating technique 69
Deming approach to quality 93
design
    activities 3
    change proposals, benefits of
        virtual organization to 124
    cost and construction management
organizations 29
    information, benefits of virtual
        organization to 124
design specification 80
design/build contractor 9
designed plan 3
designer
    improving effectiveness 14
    role 8–9
discipline leadership 68
disciplines, diverse 72, 73
disputes 69
    avoidance 45
    resolution 45

empowerment 90
engineer
    as designer 35
    role in temporary organization 51
    specialist, as supplier members of

team 77–8
exposing technique 69

failure
    missing parts in system and 94–5
    success and 41–4, 56–8
    as team members 40–1
financial forecast 23
firm-to-firm relationship 99–100
forming stage of teams 66

Gantt chart 111
generic inputs to business system
    95–7

human relationship theory
    building and leading teams 65–70
    diverse cultures 64–5
    diverse people 60–4

implicit culture 105
information
    communication of 116–19
    computer technologies and 120–3
    definition 116–19
    sharing knowledge 119–20
information access/exchange 95, 96,
    97, 98
information culture 125
information exchange 115–25, 190–1
in-house company projects 54
International Association of Project
    Managers 202

Keirsey temperament sorter 195,
    198–200

leadership, passionate 90
limited-liability companies 25
linking technique 69

MACE 37
marketing, key principles 29–30
metaphors, client organizations as 74
Myers–Briggs test 62, 63
Myers–Briggs type indicator 195,
    198–200

net arrangement 108, 109
neuro-linguistic programming (NLP)
    analysis 62, 63
New Engineering Contract (NEC) 51
norming stage of teams 67

objectives, firm 99
objectives, organizational 46–7
    harmonization of firm's and
        client's 47–9
organization, firm 99
organizational resources, failure of 42
organizational strategy 53–4
    agreeing 54–6

partnering 6, 49, 98, 101, 188
peeking technique 69
people skills/knowledge 95, 96, 98
performance standards/measures 95,
    97, 98, 99
performing stage of teams 67, 71
permanent organizations, essential
    features 104–7
permanent vs temporary nature of
    project 36–40
person culture 108
personal logic 66
personalities, diverse 64
personnel, failure of 42
Pert chart 111
policy, firm 99
power culture 105, 106, 108
preferred thing style (PTS) 62–3
Private Finance Initiative (PFI) 16
problems, organizational
    start of 44–5
    types 45
project management, rise of 66
project management organizations 29
project manager
    improving effectiveness 14
    role 5, 8, 66
    role in temporary organization 51,
        52–3
project objectives 46–7
project process 5

quality assurance (QA) systems 93,
    109–11
quality plan 99, 110

records 99
responsibilities, firm 99
role culture 105, 106, 108

self-perception analysis 61–2
Simons Construction 37
specialist trade contractor
    improving effectiveness 14
    as key team member 80–2
    role 9, 35
specialist trade contractor
    organizations 29
stakeholders 72, 190
    direct and indirect involvement of
        82–3
statistical process control (SPC) 93
storming stage of teams 67, 71
subcontractor 9
supplier organizations 29
supplier team members 75

task culture 106, 108, 109
task-orientated approach 113
team-building 65–70
team leadership 62, 65–70
    role of 71
    stages 67
team members 8–9
    diverse people 60–4
    supplier 75
team spirit 187–8, 191
teams
    definition 3–4
    history 3–4
teamwork
    'payoff' 15–16
    place in construction project 8
temple arrangement 108
temporary organization 189
    aim, objectives and ethos 112–13
    arrangement, culture and agenda
        107–8
    direction and management of 50–3

matching project objectives 107–9
organizational implications 49–50
vs permanent nature of
    project 36–40
theory X(T) 18
theory Y(T) 18
three circle needs model 4
Total Quality Management (TQM) 93
training programme 92, 201–15
    aim 202
    assessment and affiliations 213
    basis of curriculum 202–5
    course curriculum 205–10
    course management 214–15
    course philosophy 202–5
    course tutors' CVs 213–14
    projects used for learning 210–12

workbook used for practice
    application 212–13
transferring technique 69

undiagnosing technique 69

virtual teams 123–4

web arrangement 108
whole business system
    defining 91–8
    designing construction project as
        98–101
work breakdown structure
    (WBS) 111
work process/procedure 95, 96, 97,
    98
work standard 99